The
Future of Russia

HARRY BRAVERMAN *The*

Future of Russia

THE MACMILLAN COMPANY, NEW YORK

COLLIER-MACMILLAN LIMITED, LONDON

Acknowledgment is gratefully given for permission to reprint copy-righted material:

To Doubleday & Company Inc., and the author for the selections from *House Without a Roof* by Maurice Hindus;

To the editors of *Survey* for a portion of "Diversions and Distractions," by David Allchurch, *Soviet Survey*, October–December, 1958, and for the selection by Alfred G. Meyer, *Survey*, October, 1961;

To Bertram D. Wolfe for the selection from his *Communist Totalitarianism*, Boston, Beacon Press, 1961;

To the United States Information Agency for a portion of the article by Bertrand de Jouvenel in *Problems of Communism*, January–February, 1960.

© *Harry Braverman 1963*

First printing

The Macmillan Company, New York
Collier-Macmillan Canada, Ltd., Toronto, Ontario

Library of Congress catalog card number: 63–15278

Printed in the United States of America

To my mother
and the memory
of my father

Acknowledgments

My sincere thanks to Isaac Deutscher, Jules Geller, Robert Heilbroner, Adolph Lowe, and Richard Seaver, who read the manuscript and offered many helpful suggestions and criticisms, without necessarily sharing my views. A special word of thanks is due Emile Capouya, formerly Senior Editor of the Macmillan Company, at whose suggestion an article was expanded into a book, for his encouragement and help at all stages of the work. My appreciation also, for the help of my wife Miriam and my son Tommy.

H.B.

Contents

Introduction

Books about the future of the Soviet Union are
not rare on our library shelves. They were being written
ten, twenty, and even thirty and more years ago. Among
them are some which may still be read with profit. But on
the whole, the business of predicting Russia's fate has
been a thankless and harried one. It is still not much less
so today, in the polemical atmosphere of the cold war that
makes objectivity so difficult. But for a number of reasons,
some of the obstacles have been reduced. I refer not only
to the vastly increased flow of information, as a result of
the lessening of Soviet secrecy and the greatly expanded
work of Western scholars, but to another and more important factor as well.

In the long night of Stalin's reign, it was hard to
visualize a Soviet future differing from the nightmarish
and seemingly interminable present. Great changes were
apparent from the statistics of Soviet industrial development, which were startling even if one discounted them
heavily. But there were few other signs of forward evolution. In fact, the Soviet Union appeared to be undergoing
a retrogression, abandoning its early socialist idealism; all
the progress seemed to be backward.

In these circumstances, it seemed incredibly remote,
abstract, and unrealistic to speak of an eventual Russian

social evolution. Instead, discussions about an omnipotent totalitarianism which had cut off history from all its natural paths of development and which could manipulate past, present, and future with equally unchallengeable authority seemed more to the point. There was much of this sort of reasoning, and—especially after the rise of Hitlerism—there were even attempts to link national developments with global theories holding that mankind had at last succeeded in making for itself an iron prison preventing all further movement.

Today, after a decade of swift and often astounding changes in the Soviet world, much of this looks very different. From a country that seemed, despite industrial and educational progress, to live in a state of frozen immobility, the U. S. S. R. has suddenly become a highly volatile society. Western thinking has consequently begun to change. In place of a dead certitude that, short of outside intervention, nothing much would happen in Russia other than a deepening of the darkness, there is now a feeling of a profusion of possibilities, exciting and incalculable prospects of change. "Mr. Khrushchev has grasped and is shaking the roots of Soviet society," wrote the Moscow correspondent of *The New York Times* at the close of the 22nd Congress of the Soviet Communist Party which met in October, 1961. "There are few here daring enough to predict where his boldness will lead ultimately."

Much has been written in the last decade stressing the limits of change in Russia. But we have seen Western commentators forced repeatedly to move these bounds outward as new events rendered them obsolete. The truth of the matter is that *we do not know the limits of change in the U. S. S. R.* We have seen changes breed resistance on the part of elements of Soviet society, but they also breed more changes. A powerful dynamic is evidently at work, and while it is subject to many restraints, it will carry the country far from where it was at the start of the fifties, when Stalin died. Thus, unless one's purpose is chiefly propagandistic, it makes little sense to belittle the changes in Soviet society. It is time to take full cognizance of the fact that Russia, no longer restrained in the Stalinist strait jacket, is responding to the new conditions created by four decades of industrialization and modernization.

▲   ▲   ▲

The Soviet leaders have recently presented the world with fairly detailed long-range projections for the country, in the form of a new Communist program intended to cover the next two decades. Are these of any value to the would-be interpreter of Russia's future? Presumably they are, but they must be used critically—in a double sense. If we question the ability of the regime to fulfill all of its promises in the economic field, we should also question its ability to make Russia's political and cultural future little more than a continuation of the present paternalistic, manipulative, and bureaucratic present. There are thus some dependable forecasts to be drawn from the regime's plans, and some things for which they form a very unreliable guide. We can roughly distinguish between the two areas in the following way.

Much of Russian economic and social development necessarily follows a central plan. Quantities, priorities, investment, prices, are not chiefly dependent on the blind play of forces in the market, but are subject to decision by specialists and planning bodies set up for the purpose.

Accordingly there is much that can be predicted by a relatively simple process of extrapolation from past experience and a reading of Soviet plans, modifying sensibly on the basis of what we know about the difficulties as well as the possibilities. We might call this the *static* element in any forecast of Russia's future.

The *dynamic* element is harder to assess, and also far more important in the areas that have to do with the quality of life: politics, culture, social ideology, personal and community values. Here we encounter imponderables that either do not appear in the plans of the regime or cannot really be planned. The picture of the future in these fields, as formed under present conditions of Soviet ideology and opinion, may have little reality two or three decades hence. Khrushchev's view of the affluent Soviet society as "highly organized" along present lines, and of the future political system of Russia as substantially that of today with peripheral modifications, is a true reflection of the limited horizon of the Soviet elite and, in a sense, of all current Soviet thinking. Tomorrow's politics are likely to reflect a totally altered situation and mentality. From this point of view Khrushchev's political plan, generous though he may feel it to be in its promises of liberalization and communal self-government, may prove inadequate to meet the currents of self-reliance, ideological ferment, and political skepticism likely to course through the new Russia that is being created year by year. Here we are dealing with the unintended consequences of the vast social revolution still under way.

It is true that Russia is ruled by dictators, but if history teaches anything it is the vanity of trying to dictate to future generations. Above all, the Soviet Union's history has exemplified this. With his last breath Lenin decreed the removal of Stalin. Yet within a few years, the very personal traits which Lenin found so objectionable in their mildest form had been imposed on the whole of Russia as a veritable system of government. Stalin, for his part, spared neither blood nor treasure to ensure that the country remain a land of the security police in which his name would forever be hallowed. Yet almost before the embalmer had drawn the blood from his veins, his own devoted followers and heirs had begun to obscure his memory as a prelude to assailing it in the harshest terms and reversing many of his policies.

With these examples before us, it is foolish to predict the future of the Soviet Union entirely from the plans of its present oligarchs. The surprising things that have happened before can happen again. We must look rather to the massive interior processes and their consequences for the answer. If we can find a sure guide anywhere, it will be in the unprecedented pace of industrialization, the rapid modernization, the cultural transformation, and the interplay between these forces and the institutions which both assist and hinder them.

▲   ▲   ▲

This book deals exclusively with the internal developments we may expect in the Soviet Union. It does not touch on foreign policy or international relations, which lie beyond its scope. Obviously, abstracting Russia from a world in which it plays so major a role introduces an element of distortion into any forecast. But Russia's relation to the world is a vast subject, and I have thought it better to omit it from consideration in the interest of exclusive attention to internal development.

It has not been my purpose to write a comparison of East and West, or to set up another balance sheet for the contest between the Soviet Union and the United States. This book is concerned with Soviet society, and if occasional references are made to the West, the purpose is to elucidate by comparison or contrast, and by measuring against the familiar, to make the unfamiliar plain.

The implicit assumption of any such book as this one is that there will be no major war, no nuclear holocaust, cutting across the process of social change. Any predictions based on the prospect of such a war would have to be written in a calculus of death difficult to devise and still harder to face. If the world is to escape disaster, both sides must forego correcting what each regards as the errors or oversights of history by an appeal to arms. In the present nuclear context, such an attempt by either side would correct history by abolishing it. If this book contributes in any measure toward a new way of looking at Russia as an evolving society of human institutions, and thus helps to replace blind rage with understanding, it will have more than fulfilled its author's intentions.

The
Future of Russia

What Is the Soviet Union?

Soviet institutions were not shaped by a malevolent desire to plague the West, but as an answer to problems raised by the breakdown of a society under the impact of the First World War. Most Westerners remain convinced that the revolution which took Russia out of the war, the institutions established for mending the tattered social fabric, and the measures taken for rapid industrialization were profoundly unfortunate. Important as that issue is, its interest has now become chiefly historical. The deed is irreversible. It is time now to begin to understand the revolutionary implications of what has been created.

As the enormous hardships recede into history and the appalling terror is eased, the outlines of achievement emerge more clearly. In an astonishingly short space of time the Soviet Union has substantially mastered three giant tasks:

1. Creation of an urban society in place of the previously rural one. This has been made possible by an agri-

cultural system which, while grossly deficient by Western standards, has managed to feed a growing population by the labor of an ever-shrinking proportion of the labor force.

2. Industrialization of the economy on the basis of current industrial techniques and advanced scientific knowledge.

3. Alteration of the social physiognomy of the nation to conform to the immense new needs. This has called for successfully assimilating an illiterate peasant mass to the needs of modern industry, and bringing into being a large class of professionals and technicians—a social revolution of universal impact.

Agrarian revolution and urbanization, industrialization, and the creation of a new social structure: this is the trinity long familiar to the West as the essence of its own modern history. This evolution, which required centuries elsewhere, was compressed into decades in Russia. Its most striking feature is thus its rapidity—its aspect of a historic leap. But bound up with this there is an even more important characteristic: Russia has used a socialist framework to accomplish what was done elsewhere by capitalism.

The anomaly of the Russian revolution is that, taking place under the leadership of the most revolutionary and intransigent wing of the pre-World War I socialist movement, it conquered a country least prepared of all the major nations of Europe for the society that socialists hoped to build. Socialism, by its own definition, was conceived as a society more advanced in every way than capitalism, using the latter as a foundation but transcending its limitations. The Bolshevik victors in the revolution and civil war could install some socialist institutions—

state ownership of industry and trade—but found it impossible to give them the content which they, in common with all socialists, had envisaged.

Having created a social-economic structure of an unprecedented kind, the Bolsheviks found themselves precariously straddling an enormous chasm between institutions and national heritage. They were obliged to enter upon a venture unmatched in the full range of human history—the attempt to create a country suited to the new structure. We know of many instances where partially successful attempts were made to give a more advanced content to backward and outmoded institutions. Even this has always proved difficult; how much more difficult, then, to accomplish the opposite, to bring into being a new industry, new agriculture, even a new population suited to a social system conceived as ahead of its times. In the light of this extraordinary situation, it is hardly surprising that Soviet society presents so many contradictory features, and that it fits so badly into pat schemes of social evolution. If there is an evolutionary hierarchy for societies, the position occupied in it by Russia remains ambiguous.

But we are led to ask the question: What will happen within the next decade or two, when the massive preparatory stages end? The Soviet Union will inevitably complete the "capitalist" stage—that of duplicating the achievements of its rival system—sometime in the not too distant future. It will at last possess a social and industrial structure of the kind which it alone, of all the major powers of Europe, lacked when the revolution occurred. If Russia or socialism has anything truly new or superior to offer, we can only then begin to look for it to emerge.

Up until now, the impact of Soviet economic institutions upon the people of the unindustrialized parts of the globe, who are casting about so feverishly for a way to manage their own modernization, has most often been stressed. But we must soon begin to give thought not just to the ascent but to the result. We are witnessing the emergence of an industrial society that manages its affairs in a basically different way from every industrial society heretofore known. From this point of view, what should begin to interest us is not Russia's impact upon the under-developed countries, but her impact upon the most advanced industrial countries of the West.

Reaching industrial maturity, not only does the Soviet Union look back upon an unusual path for achieving it, but comes equipped with a novel set of institutions for managing it in the future. The monopoly over the affluent society will sooner or later be broken. We will get a chance to see how a different kind of society may be built around the factory, the research laboratory, the urban metropolis —all the typical aspects of the industrial world. In 1958, a leading American specialist in Russian affairs anticipated this theme, which we can be sure will engage the attention of ever larger numbers of analysts, when he wrote: "One thing certainly is that, separate from the plane of moral judgment, it is necessary for us to take the full measure of the Soviet system as an alternative form of the organization of society in the age of industrialism."[1] Let us hope there remain few in the West so smug in their belief that we have the perfect answer to all the problems of the age of industrialism that they will refuse the opportunity for a sighting from this new vantage point.

▲   ▲   ▲

If we accept this concept that with the completion of the difficult ascent a new stage of Soviet history opens up, it becomes much easier to understand what Isaac Deutscher has called the "Khrushchev Interregnum."[2] When Stalin died in 1953, the basic task of duplicating the achievements of capitalism had not been completed. Indeed, it is far from finished yet; more decades will undoubtedly have to pass before capitalism's industrial, cultural, and social feats are matched on all major levels. But economic gains and cultural transformations had already been sufficient to shake the para-military forms which Stalin had imposed on Soviet society in pursuit of rapid industrialization.

The economy had grown so rapidly that it was suffering from its successes: it could no longer be organized and operated efficiently by stubborn adherence to old administrative and planning procedures. Stalinist thought, with its rigid dogmas, archaic mystiques, and pervasive falsity, clashed at every point with the new industrial society, the widespread educational-cultural revolution that had already taken place, and the need for fresh policies in every field. The low standard of living and frightful housing conditions cried out for dramatic attack before they produced an upheaval in the population. Agriculture was in a terrible impasse that threatened the entire economic structure. At the same time, Soviet development had already brought into being many of the resources—human and material—for an attack on these critical problems.

That Stalin's death represents one of the crucial turning points of modern history will no longer be questioned by anyone. But unless we accept with Khrushchev the all-explaining theory of the "cult of personality," it is too much to assume that Stalin's removal from the scene was the sole cause of all that followed. It is a remarkable fact

that in the days immediately following Stalin's death all
the leaders without exception seemed to be trying to dis-
sociate themselves from the policies and reputation of the
dead dictator. Even Beria took the lead in appeals for a
new Soviet legality, and the reversal of the case of the
Kremlin doctors was announced by his Ministry.

The haste with which Stalin was abandoned by all his
former subordinates shows how great was the pressure
for an end to the Stalin era in politics and economics. It is
clear that the upheaval in post-Stalin Russia is associated
with his death only as an explosion is connected with a
fuse. The old structure had been mined by forces far
stronger than the pressure in Stalin's blood vessels. Even
had he been a young and vigorous man, Stalin could not for
much longer have delayed the onset of a new stage of
Russian history.

In this transitional stage, the Stalinist past is in many
ways being continued by Stalin's successors, but in important respects it is being repudiated and transcended.
The Khrushchev Interregnum reflects both the achievements and limitations, the heritage of backwardness and
the rich possibilities, of Soviet society. This fact gives to
the regime's policies in every field a double or contradictory aspect. Needless to say, it complicates the task of
the conscientious analyst. But it is in one way most helpful
to anyone trying to shape a forecast for Soviet society.
Certain possibilities of the Stalin era have become actu-
alities in the Khrushchev era. Because of this, and because
so many problems have been discussed frankly before the
world, and so many fresh voices have been raised among
the intelligentsia and the younger generation, we can now
begin to picture the future of Soviet society with some assurance that our preview is not entirely fanciful. Possibilities of development have opened up which, only a few

years ago, would have been thought impossible and were, in fact, met with extreme skepticism when they were suggested. Despite its major bonds with the past, the Khrushchev Interregnum is in itself a forecast of things to come. Properly interpreted, the tendencies it has exhibited should offer realistic guidance to the future of Russia.

The most striking aspect of Soviet development has been a prodigious capacity for economic growth. Since that is fundamental to everything else, we must begin with this subject.

C H A P T E R   II

The State Replaces
the Capitalist:
Economic Growth

"Accumulate! Accumulate! That is Moses and all the prophets!" wrote Marx in the first volume of *Capital*. "Accumulation for accumulation's sake, production for production's sake, this was the formula by which the classical political economists gave expression to the historical mission of the bourgeois period."[1]

But what if "the historical mission of the bourgeois period" is performed by nonbourgeois means? What if, in place of the capitalist, the state industrializes the nation? It should not surprise us to find that accumulation, the private religion of the capitalist world, became the state religion of the Soviet world. In the early thirties a leading Soviet economist exemplified this by writing: "Heavy industry which produces the means of production must always outstrip the development of other branches of the economy, including light industry. This holds not only under conditions of the reconstruction period but also under conditions of the developed, classless society."[2] How far is this from the "formula by which the classical political economists gave expression to the historical mission of the bourgeois period"?*

Like the capitalist, in some ways far more than the capitalist, Soviet society is enthralled by the powerful logic of the geometric progression. No miser in the pages of Balzac, no real-life Rothschild with a hunger for compound interest, ever exceeded the passion for the compound rate of growth that has seized the U. S. S. R. Where the capitalist passion for accumulation gripped individuals who gained scope to exercise it in one way or another, with the Soviets the passion is all-embracing, national, systematic, planned. The sciences and technologies of the modern era are tapped exhaustively, and the potentialities of modern production are pointed toward a logic always dreamed of but never attained in the Western countries where they were born.

▲   ▲   ▲

From both national and individual points of view, economic growth should proceed faster than growth of population and thus make available a surplus which may be used for pursuing national goals or increasing individual welfare. With the Industrial Revolution this became possible on a significant rather than on a miniscule scale. Not that the gains shown each year in per capita produc-

---

* However, as basic industrialization nears completion, this emphasis is beginning to give way. In his report on the new party program at the 22nd Congress, Khrushchev cited Lenin: ". . . means of production . . . are not manufactured for their own sake, but only because more and more means of production are demanded by the branches of industry manufacturing articles of consumption."

tion were large; on the contrary, they were surprisingly small. But, like compound interest, the effects of these small accretions over long periods of time were, as we know, extremely large.

Calculations for the nineteenth century, long before the present statistics of national product and income were devised or kept, are necessarily unreliable, but various careful attempts have been made to compile them in recent years. Dr. Raymond Goldsmith, a specialist in national-income analysis, has presented estimates for the United States going back 120 years, and although they can hardly be taken as exact, they are certainly of the general order of magnitude of the real figures. They are worth considering, for they offer an idea of the pace of American industrialization, which may serve as some standard of comparison with the Russian.[3]

For the entire period, 1839 to 1959, Dr. Goldsmith found an average rate of growth for the gross national product of 3½ percent a year. When he deflates this figure to take account of population growth—in other words, calculates the rate of growth per capita—he gets 1⅝ percent a year. Correcting for some statistical inadequacies, Dr. Goldsmith feels this is more accurately about 1¾ percent a year.

Breaking this long period down into several shorter ones yields a surprising result. Dr. Goldsmith finds, contrary to popular supposition, that the per capita rate of growth in earlier periods was not significantly higher than in later. While overall increases were much higher—in the decades from 1839 to 1879 for example—so also was population growth. His estimates show that (apart from spurts lasting under a decade) the long-term rate of growth per person was no higher in the nineteenth century than it has been in the twentieth—between 1½ and 2 percent a year.*

This percentage may seem small, but compounded annually over a long period of time, it has produced great changes in the American standard of living. Dr. Goldsmith points out that the British and Americans started from about the same general level of living standards in 1840, and that the British annual rate of per capita increase in output was apparently only about one-half of one percent smaller than the American. Yet this small difference, extended over the 120-year period, has sufficed to give Americans an average per capita product which may today be as much as double that of Englishmen.

The following pages will make an effort to present what we know about Russian growth rates. At this point we will only say that the Soviet economy is now apparently growing at somewhat more than 5 percent annually per capita. In the light of the foregoing figures for American per capita growth, this rate is nothing less than startling. It is obviously most important to see whether this is a true rate of growth, whether it is maintained over long periods of time, and whether it is likely to continue in the future. It will also be interesting to try to find some explanation for the phenomenon.

▲ ▲ ▲

* The actual figures: from 1839 to 1879, an annual growth rate of about 4¼ percent, but a population growth of 2⅝ percent; 1879 to 1919, annual growth of 3⅝ percent, population growth 1⅞ percent; 1919–1959, growth of 2⅞ percent, population increase of 1¼ percent annually. In each period, subtracting the population increase from the percentage of growth gives a per capita rise of 1⅝ or 1¾ percent a year.

Western experts, by and large, have not in the past accepted Soviet claims of economic growth. Up until several years ago they had the exaggerated statistical peaks of the Stalin period to contend with. More recently this problem has tended to diminish, and Western economists generally accept the validity of at least the basic Soviet statistics of the fifties and early sixties. Disagreements having to do with statistical concepts—mainly, the use of index numbers and the method of figuring national income—still exist. But as statistics have become increasingly reliable, and as the Soviet economy enters into a stage where conceptual difficulties are reduced for statisticians, Soviet statistics and the independent estimates of Westerners have drawn closer together.

However, the calculation of economic growth is by no means an easy task, and Western experts tend to disagree even among themselves. The estimates vary for a number of reasons. Accustomed as we are to figure growth readily by a money sum, we are not always aware that this handy expedient sometimes conceals as much as it explains, even in the West, where money prices, under market conditions, have much more meaning than in Russia. The arbitrary nature of Soviet prices has thrown Western economists back on the more substantial method of calculating from actual production figures, but this has brought them face to face with the problem of assigning an overall numerical value to an output that consists of a wide range of products rapidly changing with the changing structure of the economy. How are we to compare the size of Russian output today with that of the twenties if Russia is now producing a variety of industrial products which then did not exist at all?

Different estimates are thus likely to be arrived at. It is not my purpose to try to decide among them, or to try to settle on figures significant to the last decimal point. We can record the varying estimates of a wide range of Western scholars and from them draw a consensus. What is important is that we arrive at some idea of the general magnitudes involved and do our rough calculations within that range. For any realistic purposes of trying to assess the economic future of the U. S. S. R., that is sufficient.

When we discuss the possibilities for the Soviets to continue their high rate of growth, we will furnish more exact details of the estimates by Western experts, but for the present suffice it to say that most of them find the Soviet Union has been growing at a rate of about 7 percent a year.* An economy that grows at this rate will just about double its national product every decade (the exact doubling rate is 7.18 percent annually).

On the basis of so phenomenal a rate, Soviet output now, four and a half decades after the revolution, would be more than twenty times as large as its starting level. This is plainly incredible. But Western economists generally exclude two abnormal periods from consideration: that of World War I, the subsequent civil wars, and the reconstruction, 1917–1928; and that of World War II and the postwar rebuilding, 1941–1948. In both cases, the years omitted allow only sufficient time for the economy to regain its precatastrophe level, that of 1913 in the former case, and 1940 in the latter.

If we subtract these periods, and count only what economists call the "effective years" of Soviet growth, it was not until 1955, almost forty years after the revolution, that Russia completed two full decades of economic growth. On this basis, and accepting the 7 percent annual rate of growth given by many economists, Soviet output

* Deducting from this the current Soviet population growth of 1½ to 1¾ percent annually gives us the 5-plus percent per capita growth noted earlier in this chapter.

would have been roughly four times as large in 1955 as it was in 1928.

This check is broadly confirmed by a number of independent studies. Abram Bergson, whose exhaustive and meticulous analysis was published toward the end of 1961,[4] concluded that total output in 1955 was at least 3.5 times higher than in 1928, and at most 5.7 times higher.* Naum Jasny, a careful and highly skeptical interpreter of Soviet statistics, accepts a four-and-one-half-fold increase in Soviet national income between 1928 and 1956.[5]

These extensions of statistics back into the twenties are risky. When we get to the decade of the fifties, we are on much surer ground. Here again our 7 percent rule-of-thumb is strongly backed by most Western economists, with some going quite a bit higher. Bergson, for example, calculates the rate of growth for 1950–1955 to be 7.6 percent; there are similar results for later years in the decade from the desks of many experts, which we shall have occasion to refer to in our discussion of economic prospects for the U. S. S. R.

▲   ▲   ▲

From a strictly economic standpoint, the mechanics of this rapid velocity are well understood in the West. First and foremost is the high rate of investment. Total

* The large spread between the upper and lower limits is due to the so-called index-number problem. Widely varying results are possible, depending on whether one takes a base year at the start or end of the period, because of the great change in the nature of the goods produced by the economy. Neither method is right per se; each actually answers a different question. For a very clear elucidation of the index-number problem as it applies to the Soviet economy, see the excellent study by Robert W. Campbell, *Soviet Economic Power*, Cambridge, Mass., 1960, pp. 41–47.

investment in the United States rarely exceeds 20 percent of the gross national product, and often falls far below this ratio. In the Soviet Union, investment rose rapidly through the industrialization period until by the early fifties it had leveled off somewhere in the neighborhood of 25 percent of the total national product, or perhaps slightly more.[6]

Second, Soviet investment has been concentrated in areas where each unit of capital brings a high return in added output. Industry, typically, is an area of investment characterized by a favorable rate of return, and the Soviet Union has put almost half of its total investment into industry in typical years, while the U.S. has used little more than a fourth in this way. Conversely, a given amount invested in housing will bring far smaller returns in increased output, and the sharp divergence between Soviet and American housing investment during much of this period is well known. The situation in this regard has altered radically for Russia in the last few years, however. Vast investments in housing have not noticeably interfered with the capacity for maintaining the rapid rate of growth. This is eloquent testimony to the new ability of the Soviets to do many big things at once instead of just one major task—an important demonstration that the Russians are in a new economic stage.

The key fact about Soviet economic growth is that it is based upon different economic institutions from those of capitalism; its motive power, regulating mechanisms, and operating rules are different. Its phenomenal rate of growth is unmatched in economic history except for short bursts in special situations. And these special cases—like that of the United States in the decade of the 1870's or Japan in the 1950's—were fortuitous, unplanned, and cannot be duplicated at will by those countries—or at least have not. Thus, as remarkable as is the pace of Soviet advance, what is even more remarkable is the fact that it is elicited on command from a set of institutions which are *sui generis*. Resources and technological factors enter into the picture, but only after this most important fact: the ability, within human and technical limits, to determine the rate and direction of economic advance.

All the experience of over four decades confirms this judgment. The persistence and uniformity of the gains are such that it is hardly possible to think of them in terms of episodic bursts. There is only one peacetime period when Russian economic growth seems to have been seriously curbed: the purge years 1937–1939, which saw a slowdown due to disorganization through terror. For the rest, nobody has yet been able to satisfactorily prove a cyclical character for Soviet economic activity, although some have tried. At most, what can be shown is a penchant for "storming" (hectic and high-pressure efforts) in the latter parts of plan periods and lag in the early parts—a troublesome phenomenon in the Soviet system, but not significant in this connection. Other difficulties and even failures plague the structure, but serious as they are, they affect the rate of growth only marginally, not in its general aspect.

We may assign the ability to determine the rate and direction of growth to "totalitarianism" or to "the superiority of a planned economy," or we may use the economist's neutral "political control of the rate of investment." But whatever we call it, it remains a capability of the Soviet system that the West has thus far been unable to duplicate, and is thus unique in all large-scale modern experience.

As we shall detail in a later chapter, the restriction of living standards and the extracting of unpaid labor looms large in any account of Soviet growth. All investment and growth in any country depend in the last analysis upon this, but the Soviet case is a particularly harsh instance because of the compression of so much investment into so short a period of time. Later on we will be in a position to discuss the extent to which living standards were kept down, and how far this need be done in the future if the same rate of growth is to be maintained.

▲   ▲   ▲

Can the Russians continue their phenomenal economic advance?

Economic growth may be reduced to the expansion of two factors: the size of the labor force and the productivity of each worker. It is clear that the labor force is bound to meet a check in growth because of the low birth rate during the war years, when some twenty million persons were killed. Yet this can hardly be so restrictive as is often assumed. An increasing number of workers is the smallest part of the overall increase in output. In its present performance, as we have seen, the Soviet economy depends upon this for under 2 percent of its 7 percent annual increase. Even cutting it in half would not greatly affect the rate of growth. Not the size of the labor force, but a large increment in year-to-year labor productivity is the key factor.

A general comparison of Russian and American output and the size of the labor force of both countries would indicate that Soviet labor productivity is something less than half of American. This is borne out by various studies and estimates. Khrushchev himself told the 21st Congress of the Soviet Communist Party that the productivity of a Russian worker is on the average 40 or 50 percent that of a worker in the United States.* A study of Soviet and United States productivity in the thirties concluded that the output per head in Soviet industry was no more than 40 percent of that in the United States.[7] One student of the problem today feels it is now not much under half, and gives interesting figures for a series of industries which show Russian per capita output ranging from less than 10 percent of American for oil-well drilling to 96.5 percent for sawmills; more typical percentages in the railroad, petroleum-extraction, electric-power, cement, and cotton-cloth industries range from 36 to 65 percent.[8]

Soviet economists claim an increase of more than 7 percent a year for their labor productivity, but Western analysts scale this down to about 5 or 6 percent, in line with their overall deflation of Russian growth claims. The twenty-year perspective outlined in the new party program adopted by the 22nd Congress calls for doubling productivity in the first decade and doubling it again in the second. This program is so ambitious that it is to be doubted it can be entirely fulfilled, although even a somewhat lesser achievement will not materially alter the perspective. As productivity is the key to the entire future so far as the economy is concerned, it is worth weighing some of the factors involved.

Up until now, in the campaign to raise the productivity of labor, the Russians have been reaping the so-called "advantages of backwardness." The huge pool of underemployed farm labor could be shifted rapidly to other occupations. In the course of this shift, the gain in

---

* This does not refer to agriculture, which is a special case and must be considered separately.

the average productivity of labor for the economy as a whole was enormous. The backwardness of applied technology gave the Russians the opportunity of incorporating Western techniques in giant chunks, without passing slowly through the developmental stages or being retarded by the slow accretion of knowledge and engineering experience.

Then, too, the Russians lived off inherited capital in certain fields, such as agriculture, transportation, and housing, carrying on what was merely a holding operation in these areas. If they are now compelled to pour investment into these sectors, for which they will get back smaller gains in output than they are accustomed to, this also represents a belated sacrifice of productivity gains. Again, as their stock of fixed capital ages, they will be forced to make heavier outlays than in the past for repair and replacement, and this will lower their *net* investment, the only part which really adds to capital stock.

These are not, however, absolute barriers. For example, the volume of rural underemployment is still very great, as we shall see in our discussion of agriculture. The Soviet Union may not be able to duplicate the technical leap it made in the thirties by imitation of the West, but it still has a certain margin for borrowing. More important, it is in a position to make a considerable technical thrust out of its own resources, something which was not yet true in the thirties. As Bergson points out in a comparison with the United States, "the Russians now have a corps of 1,750,000 professionally trained scientists and engineers, or 200,000 more than we have. Currently they are graduating from their universities 180,000 of such persons, or 75,000 more than we are graduating from ours."[9] The advantages of progress may prove superior to the advantages of backwardness.

The American level of productivity is a formidable thing. It rests not only upon science, technology, and organizational skill but also upon a distinctively American tempo which no other nation has so far been able to match. There is a physical and nervous concentration of effort unique to the United States, growing out of a unique social and economic matrix. Perhaps this should not even be called a feature of a high productivity of labor; on this point it might be useful to employ the Marxist distinction between *productivity*, which depends upon technology, and *intensity*, which concerns the amount of labor of given productivity crammed into a given space of time. The American tempo, which pervades all phases of life in the United States, involves unusual expenditure of will and energy for concentrated periods, and thus an uncommon intensity of labor.

This feature of American productivity may well turn out to be impossible to imitate in the Soviet Union, as it has generally gone unduplicated in Europe. It is unlikely that Soviet industry will be able to instill this kind of tension and drive into plant operations.* This inability may be Russia's chief handicap in its race to achieve and exceed American levels of output per worker, as there is good reason to believe the road is barred to them along this particular approach. There are, of course, other roads open.

As automation in its truest sense becomes more important in world technology, the role played by American

* A group of American unionists who visited eight Soviet factories in 1960, including automobile, meatpacking, textile, clothing, shoe, heavy machinery, and housing prefabrication plants, found the "leisurely work pace of Soviet workers . . . unexpected and puzzling. . . . In six of the eight factories the pace of work was quite slow as compared with standards that prevail in America. Only at the meatpacking plant and the shoe factory did the work pace appear to be comparable to our own practices." (Ernest Mazey, United Auto Workers, Detroit, in an unpublished memorandum.)

production-line tempo is likely to decline in importance. Machinery can take over some of the pressure that bears on muscle and nerve today, and engineering skill becomes more important than rationalization of labor in the old sense. Thus productivity has many aspects, and those who are not fully able to exploit one will try to find means to improve their exploitation of others.

The balance sheet for the future of Russian industrial growth is complicated and weighted by many factors: availability of labor and resources, scientific advances and engineering techniques, demands from the consumer sector of the economy, and so on. We may assess some of these factors, as we have attempted above, but the matter is best understood in its most general terms. Soviet growth has hitherto been dependent chiefly on the quantitative expansion of industry, which means basically the building of more industrial establishments and the conversion of more peasants into workers. They can still do much more of this, but unquestionably the nature of their problem is changing. The great new test confronting the Russian economy is one of productive efficiency in existing plants rather than creation of more large-scale industry. While the latter is still important, the emphasis is shifting from quantity to quality.

The asset they have in this completely new stage of their economic growth is leverage over the economy in the form of planning of the rate and allocation of investment. The power of this leverage should not be underestimated. While there is no doubting the difficulty of the problem they face, there is no reason to believe that it is any more difficult than the one they have already surmounted by the use of these economic controls. The task of revamping their entire economy to make it twice and three times more productive is hardly more onerous than was the enormous job of building it in the first place, and will be carried through under far less painful conditions. I see no reason to doubt its successful completion in its major aspects, although there will undoubtedly be many failures, crises, and unexpected obstacles along the way.

But one of the crucial points about this new stage of the Russian economy is that it affects their entire social fabric as well. When the regime was assembling the urban working force and impressing upon it new habits and a new way of life, coercion could and did play a major part. The race for productive efficiency cannot be run this way. Coercion must unquestionably recede into the background; in its place motivations of a different sort must be brought forward to a more prominent position: earning incentives, the pleasures of workmanship, the attractions of status, national and community pride, or other inspirations which *evoke* rather than *force* efforts. Thus in all three fields—industrial techniques, economic planning, and social conditions—Russia enters a new stage as the economy moves from its exclusive concern with massive accretions to its new concern with improving what it has built.

▲   ▲   ▲

The new program of the Soviet Communist Party calls for increasing the total output of the economy about fivefold by 1980. This is to be made up of a sixfold rise in industrial production and a three-and-one-half-fold growth of agriculture. In terms of percentages per year, this works out to about 9.4 percent annually for industry,

6.5 percent for agriculture, and 8.4 percent for the total output. As we have seen, Western estimates allow at least a 7 percent average growth rate for the Soviet economy in its "effective years." It is generally thought, however, that this growth rate was exceeded in the fifties, although there are few who think the pace can be maintained at quite this level for the next two decades. The impression is that the Soviet Union will not be able to sustain the growth rates provided in the new plan, but that it will not fall seriously below them; this impression is borne out by a survey of Western expert opinion.

One of the fullest appraisals of the twenty-year economic perspective was made by Naum Jasny.[10] Although Dr. Jasny's critique was written before the 22nd Congress and does not deal with the additional material and emendations provided at the Congress, it is one of the best that has been done. Jasny makes three major criticisms of the perspective. First, it plans too far ahead, for a time which nobody can be definite about. Second, it sets obviously absurd targets for vital items, especially in agriculture. Third, it exhibits a glaring disproportion between the targets for national income and for labor productivity.*

For the rest, Jasny finds some of the goals too high. Although he refuses to commit himself to a forecast for twenty years in the future, he feels that the economy may be able to maintain its high growth rates of the past few

---

* In this third point, Dr. Jasny has reference to what appears to be a crude error by the authors of the document in setting the rise in agricultural output at 250 percent in twenty years, while the pace of increase for the productivity of agricultural labor, which follows this ascent quite reasonably in the first ten years, shoots up sharply in the second so that it increases five- to sixfold in the twenty-year period. Obviously, as Jasny points out, such an increase in agricultural productivity per farm worker, if it is possible, accompanied by a much smaller increase in farm output, will release huge numbers of agricultural workers from the land—some ten to thirteen million, Jasny calculates—and there is no sign that the authors take this into account in the industrial-urban part of their perspective.

years in the first part of the period. Since Jasny is on record accepting a growth rate for the Soviet economy during the early fifties of as high as 9 percent,[11] this amounts to a virtual acceptance of the overall Soviet capability for the first years of the plan; later on, however, he feels that the rate of growth will have to decline somewhat as declines in the rate of increase of labor productivity set in.

Professor Alfred G. Meyer, a political scientist and specialist in communism, offers the following assessment of the prospects of economic growth as a basis for his discussion of the future of the Soviet Union:

... we shall assume the continuation of Soviet economic growth at the rate achieved in the post-war years. Some Western economists would question such an assumption. On the basis of analogies with growth rates under capitalism, they predict a leveling-off for the Soviet economy, a prediction which has been certified in the new CPSU programme. In addition, one might cite the great number of serious deficiencies which the Soviet economy still has to overcome before it rivals that of the United States: the preponderance of coal and steel over oil and chemicals; the low productivity of labour in all but a few key operations; the increasing cost of converting rural into industrial labour; the housing problem and the primitive state of the retail distribution system. The task of removing these and other deficiencies might well be so formidable as to slow down the rate of growth. On the other hand, there are factors which might speed it up even more, such as the advantages of planning by computers over the market mechanism, and the dynamic possibilities inherent in the most modern technology. It therefore seems reasonable to assume a continuation of present growth rates.[12]

The editors of *Survey*, a journal of Soviet and East European studies published on behalf of the Congress for Cultural Freedom in London, also endorse this view in a

general way: "Communism, after all, is a gigantic attempt
to change the world; great economic progress has been
achieved and more will be attained in the future. The
desire to build a better and radically different world may
not be as intense as it used to be, but the revolutionary
flame has not been completely extinguished. It is very
likely that the Soviet Union will create in the course of
time what it considers the economic preconditions for the
transition to communism."[13]

Dr. Rudolph Schlesinger, editor of *Soviet Studies*, a
quarterly edited at the University of Glasgow, finds in his
lengthy analysis of the new program no serious internal
barriers to fulfillment of the economic part of the perspective: "The availability of the material resources on
which the authors of the programme rely may be taken for
granted on the condition . . . that internal reconstruction
will not be delayed by international complications."[14] The
treatment by Rush V. Greenslade, an economist writing
on the program in the magazine of Soviet affairs published
by the United States Information Agency, divides the
prospects sharply between industry and agriculture:
"Given the priorities of the past and of the program itself,
the goal for industry appears possible of fulfillment, but
the agricultural goal seems quite infeasible."[15]

The London *Economist* also felt little doubt about the
industrial goals: "The few indicators of 1980 that are offered—such as the planned sixfold increase in gross industrial output or the crude steel capacity of 250 million
tons—are almost exact projections of rates of growth in
recent years. . . . The pledges are not quixotic, but a projection of current trends."[16] This point is strengthened by
a special correspondent of *The Times* of London, who
pointed out that the growth rates underlying the program

are slightly lower for the decade of the seventies than they are at present, by and large.[17]

We may supplement these comments on the twenty-year program with some estimates of Soviet growth possibilities made as general comments on the economic picture, without reference to the program.

Robert W. Campbell, in his *Soviet Economic Power*, accepts the validity of the seven-year plan, which ends in 1965, with some exceptions, writing: "It seems that the basic elements of the plan can probably be accomplished, though past experience raises the suspicion that there may be disappointments in such elements as housing, in agriculture, and in reduction of the work week."[18] The greatest single threat to future rapid growth, he feels, is a shortage of labor due to low birth rates in the war years. Thus he believes that a 5 percent growth per year is a "reasonable projection."*

Morris Bornstein of the University of Michigan, in his testimony before a joint Congressional committee, put the increase in the Soviet national product at 6½ to 7½ percent a year in the period 1950–1958, and felt that the five or ten years to come would show a growth rate of 6 to 6½ percent.[19] Gerhard Colm of the National Planning Association, testifying at the same committee hearings, rated the Soviet economy in the same years as increasing its national income at a rate of 8 to 9 percent a year, and his projection for the years ending in 1965 was a growth rate of 6 percent in national income and 7 to 8 percent a year in

---

* This is one of the lower projections of Soviet economic growth made by a Western specialist. In view of this it is somewhat surprising to find that Professor Campbell (together with Dr. Alexander Tarn) is responsible for one of the highest estimates on record of the present level of Soviet industrial production, which they gauged in an article for the *American Economic Review* (September, 1962) as having been 75 percent of the American level in 1960. This estimate, far exceeding the more customary guesses, aroused considerable dissent.

industrial production—in each case something like 1 or
1½ percent under Soviet projections.[20]

Finally, Abram Bergson, on the basis of his exhaustive
statistical materials, reaches somewhat similar conclusions. He assumes a small growth in the labor force up to
1975, only 1 percent a year. His various measurements for
productivity gains in the fifties, where index-number
problems disappear or are minimized, generally agree in
yielding a growth rate of 6.1 percent a year. This adds up
to a 7.1 percent rate of growth, or almost exactly the rate
needed to double output every decade. "It is not easy,"
Dr. Bergson writes, "to gauge the net of the opposing
forces that have been described. In the coming years, the
rate of growth of Soviet Russia's output per worker may
decline below its recent high level, but if so one hesitates
to assume that the reduction will soon be very consequen-
tial."[21]

The new Soviet program, which appeared after the
completion of Dr. Bergson's study and to which he makes
no reference, set its sights, it will be recalled, on an 8.4
percent annual increase, compared to the 6 or 7 percent
around which most Western predictions seem to hover.
The higher Soviet projection assumes a fractionally higher
increase in labor force than Dr. Bergson expects. On the
whole, the differences between Soviet and Western prog-
noses is about on the order of the difference between Soviet claims and Western reductions of growth estimates
for the decade of the fifties. It is not a decisive difference,
and we may conclude that Western specialists, by and
large, expect the overall growth program to be fulfilled,
although they are doubtful of results in certain fields.

▲   ▲   ▲

How large is total Soviet output now? Most of the available estimates are for the end of the fifties. At that time the Central Intelligence Agency set Soviet gross national product at about 45 percent of that of the United States, "computed on the same basis as we compute our own."[22] Harry Schwartz of *The New York Times* gives the same figure.[23] Gerhard Colm gave the proportion for 1958 as 43 percent of American output, but Morris Bornstein set it at about 46 percent in the same year. As Soviet growth has continued at an undiminished pace in the four or five years that have elapsed, while American growth has slowed down, we can see that a figure of 50 percent for Soviet output as a percentage of American is not unlikely in the early sixties.

Most commentators, Soviet and Western alike, have used these figures as the starting point for a discussion of how rapidly Soviet national output will overtake that of the United States, a pastime which is becoming the favorite guessing game of modern times. With the United States growth rate well under half the Russian, it is obvious that an intersection in the lines of output is bound to come some time in the not too distant future. If recent trends continue for as few as two to three decades, there is little question that the Soviets will catch up.

But for purposes of this analysis, and for most other realistic purposes as well, we need not play this game. The important thing to notice is that within perhaps another decade the U. S. S. R. will be producing a national product of about the size produced by the richest and most productive country in the world at the end of the fifties. Even by 1965, Soviet heavy industry, in the forefront of the drive, will be producing substantially more than did the corresponding industries of the United States in 1958.[24] Russian affluence will be comparable to that of the most developed countries of Western Europe, and second only to the United States.

It is clear that by any reasonable measure they will have immense resources to dispose of for their various national, communal, and personal purposes.

CHAPTER III

Is Agriculture the Achilles' Heel?

Some nineteenth-century political thinkers believed that Russia could skip over capitalism and jump directly into socialism. Early socialists like Herzen and Chernyshevski advocated this view. They based it upon the existence of the traditional peasant commune, the *obshchina,* a distinctive form of land tenure and village administration which seemed to them to hold out the promise of a direct transition to communal living. They thus saw in the Russian peasant the beginnings of a Russian form of socialism.

Despite the occasional celebrations of the prophetic foresight of these men, nothing remotely like this has happened. The peasantry or large parts of it, it is true, rallied to the revolution in its earliest years, defending it against attack and invasion in the civil wars of Reds and Whites. But it was at that time attracted by the Bolshevik program of expropriation of the landowners and distribution of the land to the peasants, and perhaps also animated by feelings of nationalism when the invasions came from without.

The village commune notwithstanding, ideas of socialism and communal agriculture were far beyond the horizon of the mass of the peasantry. Left to itself after the revolution, the countryside would have developed rapidly along private proprietary lines, on the petty-capitalist model, with a sharpening social differentiation between well-to-do and poor, larger owners and agricultural laborers. The years of the New Economic Policy in the mid-twenties, when the peasants were given scope to follow their bent, demonstrated this quite clearly.

Far from becoming the citadel of the revolution and the seat of a new society, as admirers of the peasant commune had dreamed, the villages have taken the very opposite part. They are to this day the least changed portions of Russian society, and partly because of innate social resistance and partly because of the policies pursued for a quarter of a century, remain the most resistant to change.

Through all the years of basic industrialization, from 1928 to Stalin's death, Soviet agriculture was little more than a holding operation. Farm production did not increase during that period by more than 30 percent, and as population went up by almost the same amount, the food supply per person was no better at the end of the period than it had been at the beginning. Considered simply as a holding operation with severely limited objectives, this in itself was a sort of success, although not one to be very proud of. All the regime proved able to do —despite its grandiose propaganda claims—was to keep farm production going with a shrinking proportion of the labor force, and to extract from the farms enough produce to feed the cities without giving much of anything in return.

Under the landowning nobility in Czarist days a considerable surplus had been siphoned off by means of the landlord-tenant relationship. Enough passed into the landowner's hands to support an aristocracy in luxury and other city dwellers in lesser style and at the same time to export as much as 10 million tons of grain a year—a huge amount, equal to about 7 percent of present grain production.

But with the revolution and the distribution of the land, the new regime no longer had a claim on the output of the farms. The old exploitative relationship had been ended. But the new government, in view of its hopes for industrialization, had an even greater need than the old for extracting part of the product from the peasant.

Its purely commercial weapons were flimsy. The impoverished cities had little to offer the peasant in return for his agricultural produce. The prolonged trial of the New Economic Policy, giving freer reign to commercial exchange, showed the hopelessness of this path from the point of view of making large resources available for speedy industrialization. Every time the regime tried to manipulate the terms of trade in order to extract more, the peasant went on strike and threatened to strangle the cities and along with them the regime.

The solution took the form of a frontal assault. Collectivization "solved" the problem by subjecting the peasants to the will of the government. But in its actual functioning it served as a collection agency for the state rather than as a superior form of agricultural organization.

"We are paying now," Khrushchev recently told an American newspaperman, "for Stalin's mistakes in agriculture."[1] The range and scale of those mistakes are awe-inspiring. Difficult enough in itself, the policy was carried through to the accompaniment of major blunders whose echoes still resound through the Soviet economy.

To start, Stalin preceded the collectivization plunge by a prolonged period of encouraging the peasants to enrich themselves, in the hope that the private prosperity of the better-off farmers would aid in the slow industrialization of the country. Few peasants got very rich, but many got rich in illusions. The violent switch to the civil-war methods of collectivization caught the peasant at the height of his resistance, filled with hopes of private enrichment and resentful of any measures to restrict him, let alone wipe out his private holding. The merits of the "rightist" or "leftist" policies are still being debated, but apart from any decision that can be reached in this dispute, what is involved here is the violent juxtaposition of *both* policies. The regime was bound to have difficulties with the peasants in any attempted collective reforms, but those difficulties were in this way intensified by the hopes and entrenched positions won during the preceding years.

As if this were not enough, the manner of introducing collectivization as a sweeping expropriation of equipment, livestock, even personal possessions was certain to heighten the resistance of the peasants—and no worthy reason has yet been adduced to show that it was necessary. The peasant was roused to a last-ditch fight. When it was all over, when millions of peasants had been deported, imprisoned, shot, when half the livestock had been killed for meat by peasants who preferred this to surrendering them to the new collectives, when agricultural production had been thoroughly disrupted and parts of the country brought to the brink of famine, the system proved unworkable. Stalin was forced in 1935 to completely revamp the collectives, make very important concessions, permitting the peasant to farm his own plot and keep a few head of livestock (with pasture rights), and allow certain administrative concessions as well.

It is in the form of this compromise that the collectivization system has continued down to the present day. We cannot say what would have been the result had the compromise been offered at the outset, but there is reason to believe that the course of events would have been far different. As it is, Soviet agriculture suffered blows from which it did not recover for two decades—the livestock population actually did not get back to the precollectivization level until the mid-fifties! And more important, the regime and peasants faced each other in mutual hostility, which from all accounts is only now being dispelled.

In the years that followed, the one-sided scale of priorities left agriculture starved for capital investment, vigorous and talented manpower, and adequate stimulus for the peasants. By simple arithmetic, less for the farm meant more for industry, but complex social and economic equations are not always soluble by simple arithmetic. It is questionable whether Soviet industrialization gained as much from the neglect and capital-starvation it imposed on agriculture as is often assumed even by observers outside the Soviet Union. The breakneck haste of the thirties and late forties left a bill which the present regime is trying hard to meet, but so badly has agriculture lagged that Khrushchev is trying to fill what often seems to be a bottomless pit. Greater haste, in the long run, might have been made more slowly.

▲   ▲   ▲

Far more intractable than political difficulties are the conditions of soil and climate that handicap Soviet agriculture. Although the U. S. S. R. is about equal in area to the continent of North America, its agricultural heartland is somewhat smaller: the so-called Fertile Triangle, traditionally bounded by lines between Leningrad in the north, Odessa in the south, and a point somewhat east of the Urals. This has now been supplemented by areas in Kazakhstan and western Siberia, amounting to perhaps a quarter of the size of the former farming region.

The limited extent of the Soviet agricultural heartland is not the major disadvantage, however. More troublesome are conditions of soil and climate that definitely weaken the validity of the comparisons often made between Russian and American agricultural output.

Despite its vast extent, the U. S. S. R. is a more northerly region than is generally realized. While all of the United States lies below the fiftieth parallel, almost all of the Soviet Union lies above it. The southernmost section of European Russia is on a latitude with Wyoming, Montana, and the Dakotas. All of Asian Russia lies above the United States' Canadian border. The taiga (northern coniferous forests) and treeless Arctic tundra cover nearly two-thirds of the entire Soviet Union. The Fertile Triangle itself has a cool semi-arid climate like that of the prairie provinces of Canada or the Dakotas. This is the most favored portion of the Soviet Union for agricultural purposes, and clearly it starts with a large handicap.

In the farming belt rainfall reaches a maximum average of 20 inches annually. By contrast, in the best agricultural regions of the United States this is a minimum. In the United States, corn cultivation is premised on an average rainfall of 20 inches and an average July temperature of 68 degrees; these conditions obtain in half of the United States. In the Soviet Union they are hardly found at all. Most of those regions having as much as 20 inches of rainfall have far colder temperatures. The warmer areas, on the other hand, are deficient in rainfall, tending to be semi-arid. Only in a tiny spot east of the Caspian Sea is there an overlap of the rainfall and temperature conditions ideally needed for corn. The Russians must therefore experiment with cold-resistant strains of corn, attempt to irrigate dry, warm areas, and for the rest, gamble extensively on weather conditions, as Khrushchev has been doing with mixed success.

The growing season is cool, short, and uncertain, and harvest time generally features cool, moist weather that adds to the hazards of farming by imperiling the crop. Soil conditions as well are anything but favorable. Permafrost covers nearly half the country. This and the adverse structure of the soil result in poor drainage, which makes both farming and building operations more difficult. The soil is deficient also in soluble plant foods; the richest black-earth areas in the southeast are in the semi-arid region and suffer from drought.

With all this, the per-acre yields of Soviet crops are much lower than in the United States. It is impossible, save by way of rough estimate, to guess how much of this is attributable to poor farming methods, inadequate fertilizer, and other human factors, and how much to the conditions of soil and climate. Obviously a good deal of the low acreage productivity comes from the latter. Corn output is estimated at less than half of American yields per acre; wheat at about two-thirds; potatoes, less than half; cotton and sugar beets also well under half. An overall estimate gives Soviet agriculture a productivity per acre of about 40 percent of that in the United States.[2]

Given this 40 percent figure, which can be raised but probably cannot be brought up to parity with American yields, we can see that apart from social systems and agricultural methods, comparisons with American farming are not entirely fair. The Russians have talked about fantastic schemes to break their natural limitations—such as vast irrigation projects beyond anything ever attempted, or shrinking the polar icecap by nuclear energy in order to raise the mean temperature of the entire land mass. But these are either fanciful or far in the future. It must be recognized that as an economic enterprise Soviet farming can succeed only within limits narrower than those imposed on many other countries.[3]

▲   ▲   ▲

Agriculture has been the scene of the most sweeping changes made by Khrushchev since Stalin's death. The energy of the attack, the commitment of resources, the audacity of the gambles taken, the management upheavals—in all these we see a revolutionary departure from Stalin's approach, which was content to make up the sordid deficiencies of Soviet farming with glowing film tributes and falsified statistics.

In the past the farm requisitions of the state were taken from the collectives at what amounted to confiscatory prices. Often, as Khrushchev pointed out, the prices paid did not suffice to cover the cost of transporting the grain to the government collection points, which was paid by the collectives. Starting shortly after Stalin's death, a series of increases was decreed; together with the boosts in farm output the collectives were spurred to achieve, these brought farm income up to almost four times its level at the time of Stalin's death, within the short space of five years. At the same time prices paid by the farmers for industrial products fell by about 20 percent. This was a major upheaval in the economic position of many collective farms, and has undoubtedly changed the perspective of rural areas considerably.

The Machine Tractor Stations, organized after collectivization to keep expensive machinery out of the hands of the collective farms and to serve as an additional government collection agency (the MTS were paid in kind), have been disbanded. Not only did these Stations make for "two masters on the land," but they also undertook much machine work for the collectives that was unnecessary, as their quotas were given to them in the form of areas processed. The farms had no control over quality, and much of the work was poorly done. Turning the machines and tractors over to the farms gives them greater autonomy, and also improves their economic position. They are relieved of the deliveries formerly required to pay for the machine and tractor work, and they are able to buy the machines out of their greatly expanded income.

By far the biggest agricultural step taken by Khrushchev, and also the most daring, is the opening up of approximately 100 million acres of virgin land in western Siberia, Kazakhstan, and other regions. Requiring enormous resources and great masses of labor and managerial staff, it is one of the most extensive efforts of the fifties, and it has been the advent of this program more than any other measure which has symbolized to the Russians and the world the end of the era of total agricultural neglect.

The Khrushchev farming program has not been the unmitigated disaster that one would gather from the tone of some Western critics. Soviet agriculture is still anything but dynamic, efficient, and economically responsive. It will take a long time before the countryside is significantly changed from its ancient degraded aspect. But output has been greatly increased by the post-Stalin reforms and investments. The increases were very sharp from 1953 to

1958, which was the peak year, and since that time have leveled off on a plateau from which they rather stubbornly refuse to ascend. This plateau, however, is high above the levels of the depressed years under Stalin.

Naum Jasny has calculated that farm output grew at the rate of 5 or 6 percent a year, on the average, from Stalin's death to 1960.[4] This is below the planned and predicted rates of growth for the period, and slightly below the regime's hopes for the next twenty years. On this score Khrushchev has been vulnerable, and his vulnerability has been exploited by Western critics and, no doubt, domestic opponents. Five or 6 percent a year, however, is a very good rate of growth indeed, and even if no more than this average is attained for a decade or two, it would revolutionize the agricultural picture.

From 1928 to Stalin's death, as we have pointed out —a full quarter of a century—farm output rose by no more than 30 percent; but in the five years after his death it jumped by at least that much; by some accounts far more. The second half of the decade of the fifties showed great gains over the first half: almost 50 percent more grain, almost two-fifths more vegetables, and a near doubling in state purchases of meat, milk, and eggs. The livestock population, which it will be recalled was barely recovered from the ravages of collectivization and thus showed a standstill over a twenty-year period, also grew considerably under the new policies: by the end of the fifties cattle and sheep herds were almost 30 percent larger than at mid-decade, and the number of pigs 73 percent higher.

All of this, as innumerable foreign observers have testified, affords the Soviet city population a much larger and somewhat more varied diet, and has given the collective farms more income, more factory goods, more capital to invest, more hope, thus permitting them to begin to stir from their ancient posture of stultification and decay.

▲   ▲   ▲

On the collective farmlands the productivity of labor is unbelievably low. In the case of grain, the most important single product, the labor input in the late fifties was 7.3 times as high as in the United States for an equal amount of crop. Potatoes took five times as much labor; sugar beets 6.2; cotton 2.3; milk 3.1; gain in weight of beef cattle 14.2 and for hogs 16.3! Khrushchev himself, in a speech of 1958, is the authority for these comparisons.[5]

These differences are so staggering that one is at a loss to know how to interpret them. In part, they are clearly due to the low yields of Soviet land described above, imposing the need to cultivate at least twice as much land for the same output as in the United States. The fact that Soviet farms use only about a third as much mineral fertilizer per acre, less than a tenth the pesticides, only about a fifth as many tractors and trucks (and infinitely fewer passenger cars, which are a great farm asset), and a quarter of the electric power available to American farms obviously also has a great deal to do with the result.

Then there is also the fact that most of the surplus of women over men resulting from wartime casualties, amounting to some twenty million, is concentrated in the rural areas; in the urban areas the number of men is only slightly lower than the number of women.[6] From this, and

from what we know about the siphoning off of the young,
the energetic, the ambitious, into the city industries and
professions, something may be conjectured about the nature of the agricultural work force.*

These are all important considerations, and go a long
way to explain the extremely low productivity of Soviet
farm labor. But one is still left with the suspicion that the
countryside is actually an area of underemployment.

The editor of the *Wall Street Journal,* in his journey
through Russia in the summer of 1962 with a group of
newspaper editors, noted this repeatedly:

> . . . the farm seemed enormously overloaded with people,
> a characteristic of every farm we saw. There are no fences any-
> where, for example, and every herd of cows or flock of sheep
> must be constantly tended. On one farm it took 17 people to
> care for 2,000 head of hogs, whereas in America that number
> can be handled easily by a man and a boy.
> The mixtures of modernity and antiquity are everywhere.
> We saw, for example, one dairy farm that had a beautiful up-
> to-the-minute milking barn, but there were a dozen people
> around getting the cows in and out.[7]

This point about labor underemployment has been
most sharply made by a British economist who has written
the best introductory textbook on the Soviet economy, and
the example he gives is very instructive:

* "The thing Shukhov didn't get at all was what his wife wrote about
how not a single new member had come to the kolkhoz since the war.
All the youngsters were getting out as best they could—to factories in
the towns or to the peat fields. Half the kolkhozniks had not come back
after the war, and those who had wouldn't have anything to do with
the kolkhoz—they lived there but earned their money somewhere outside.
The only men in the kolkhoz were the gang boss, Zakhar Vasilyevich,
and the carpenter, Tikhon, who was eighty-four, had married not long
ago, and even had children already. The real work in the kolkhoz was
done by the same women who'd been there since the start, in 1930."—
One Day in the Life of Ivan Denisovich by Alexander Solzhenitsyn, New
York, 1963, p. 45.

As might be expected, this was most easy to observe in *kolkhoz* agriculture, in which, since the total remuneration of labour was independent of the amount of labour expended, the marginal cost of using extra labour appeared, from the standpoint of the management, to be *nil* (the more so as the additional labour would be at the expense of working on the private plot). Only thus can one explain the deployment of 70 peasants in two shifts (total: 140) on one grain-thresher, and this form of using machinery and peasants actually won a Stalin prize![8]

Clearly the Stalin prize was awarded not for ingenuity in saving labor, but for ingenuity in deploying a horde of really unnecessary peasants around a machine operation.

All these facts indicate that the low productivity figures for farm labor derive at least in part from the existence of a surplus labor force which is reckoned into productivity figures. Some of the gap between Soviet and more normal productivity levels could undoubtedly be closed at once by a reduction in the number of peasants, which would not hinder farm operations at all in many cases. Of course such a reduction is not so easy.

What all this means, in other words, is that the countryside is still a reservoir of population and labor, which will be drawn upon as conditions for its employment and housing in the cities are prepared. This population reservoir is maintained in the only way possible: on the farms, at minimal cost and often no more than nominal employment. The same has been true of every country in its process of switching from a farm to a factory economy and from a predominantly rural to a predominantly urban composition, although perhaps not to the same degree as in Russia. This is an important consideration for the answer to the questions posed about the ability of Russian industry to continue its expansion, and is one reason to think that Russian industrial growth will not soon meet a check because of manpower difficulties.

▲   ▲   ▲

From any point of view other than that of survival, or of a holding operation enabling the country to industrialize, Soviet agriculture has been an almost unqualified failure. Unlike the remarkable performance of the nationalized industries, the collectivized farms have until recently shown little ability to expand output, and even after the recent spurt to a better level of performance, the resistance to further improvement is apparently strong. The Soviet high command is repeatedly concerned with agricultural policy, explaining disappointing results, altering policies and shifting personnel, increasing capital investment. With all this, they have still been unable to make a really decisive change in the situation.

The hallmark of Russian development since the revolution is the use of socialist forms of economic organization to accomplish the transformation wrought in other countries by capitalism. While this has worked phenomenally well in industry, it has not worked at all in agriculture. Little transformation has yet been wrought in the countryside, which throughout most of Russia remains sunk in its immemorial lethargy and backwardness.

Part of the reason is of course that for three decades the country was run on an exclusive industrial priority. It was a case of one thing at a time. But this neglect is only part of the story. The collective farm system, left to itself, proved unsuited to developing anything, as it lacked drive, initiative, and internal resources. Khrushchev has immortalized this aspect in a hundred speeches and resolutions under the clumsy rubric, "the violation of the socialist principle of material incentives." We might more fittingly call it "the violation of the capitalist principle of material incentives," but whichever system claims the honor of owning the appeal to human acquisitiveness, the fact remains that the peasant had and still has little personal reason to throw himself into efforts on the collective's lands, and every reason to save himself for his own plot. A genuinely socialist incentive to work, in the form of community feeling or even enlightened and farsighted self-interest, is barely present throughout much of the Soviet culture, and least of all on the farms.

In the cities and industrial enterprises the regime was able to provide the driving power partly by its wages system, sharply graduated according to output, and partly by a Draconian labor discipline. On the farms money incentives were almost entirely absent, and coercion, in the very nature of the operations performed—their dispersal, the impossibility of close supervision, the greater need for individual initiative—was bound to be practically ineffective.

Capitalist development of agriculture, particularly in the United States, drew enormous dynamism from the economic system. It is not for nothing that the individually owned farm—or factory—was, even according to Marx's ideas, history's chosen instrument for developing modern levels of proficiency. The impersonal and ruthless coercion of the marketplace offered the incentive of a higher income to those developing greatest productive efficiency, or, to state the matter another and often more realistic way, imposed a sentence of death upon enterprises that lagged for any reason. This drew from many farmers, as from other entrepreneurs, a self-imposed labor discipline and efficiency drive, in running their enterprises with either family labor or hired labor, that no external coercion can match or even approach.

In industry the Soviet system is today troubled by the absence of such an agency of regulation and coercion as the marketplace. But this is relatively a secondary problem, since the pace and direction of economic development can be forced by various significant incentives and by planning, investment control, and the dictation of national priorities. In agriculture, however, the system has little to put in place of the market.

Thus Soviet farming has been carried on under conditions of monumental indifference on the part of the peasant to the level of output, the productivity of labor, the condition of buildings and equipment, the care of livestock, or most other things concerning the collective farm. Such love as he has for his work he has lavished on his small kitchen plot and private livestock, with the result that, occupying a tiny proportion of Soviet land, these remnants of the compromise of 1935 have played a disproportionate role in Soviet agriculture, supplying through the private market large percentages of the meat and dairy foods consumed by the Russian people.

Is a successful and well-developed agriculture, fully mechanized and electrified, based upon modern towns offering the amenities of modern civilization and culture, and able to repeat its routinized seasonal tasks without undue effort or an air of crisis, conceivable on the basis of a collectivized or socialized system? There is no reason to reject the possibility out of hand. In such a situation, the employment of labor on the same basis as in factories is not necessarily a drawback, as many large factories in the field in the United States and elsewhere demonstrate. This is merely another way of saying that the socialist structure may be best suited to build on the achievements of capitalism, and not as a substitute for them. It has failed to meet many of the tests in agriculture for that reason, but it will confront a new and favorable situation if, by dint of heavy investment and close attention, rural culture is elevated to the requisite modern level.

▲   ▲   ▲

Russia has elements of two other social systems on the land, and both of these have displayed greater vigor than the collective farms.

The peasant has, until recently, been putting in about a third of his labor time on his tiny kitchen plot. These plots are normally only one-fourth of a hectare (three-fifths of an acre); yet by hand labor, without any of the advantages of large-scale operation supposed to derive from collectives, the peasants have wrung from them almost a third of the agricultural output of the country in a typical year! This mere 4 percent of the cultivated land produced in 1959 over half the meat and potatoes and almost all the eggs for the U. S. S. R.[9] The fact that the peasants got more than 60 percent of their income from private plots in 1957 while investing only a third of their labor time may help to explain this devoted tillage.[10] Politically, however, a wholesale return to private farming is, of course, still regarded—and likely to continue to be viewed —as incompatible with the formulated goals of the regime.

The state farms have grown considerably in impor-

tance in recent years, and now occupy in the neighborhood of one-third of the Soviet tilled area. A state farm is
run like a factory, with hired labor, as distinguished from
the collective farm, which is a form of co-operative. Operated on a wage and salary basis, rather than with the
residual shares in profits used as a payment system on the
collective farms, they provide a higher and more assured
income to their labor force, and their productivity shows
the effects of this and other advantages. In the cases of
grain, cotton, and milk, it amounts to almost double the
productivity of labor on collective farms; for potatoes and
sugar beets, better than four times as much; and for livestock almost seven times as much! This brings productivity up to levels which bear some comparison with American farming—still far below, but about comparable to the
ratio for Soviet industrial labor productivity as a percentage of American, which, it will be remembered, is
something like half. This is a far cry from the collective-
farm level, which is typically 10, 15, or 20 percent of the
American.[11]

While the mind of the Soviet peasant is not really
known on this matter, it has long been assumed from the
history of collectivization that he would resent the further
step of being transformed into a worker on a state farm,
and prefers the semiprivate status of the farm co-operative.
This, however, is only an assumption, and, it seems to me,
no longer a realistic one. His status is by now far closer
to proletarian than peasant, and he must forego the advantages of steady and uninterrupted pay for uncertain
and generally lower returns in the form of a share in the
residual income after all costs and investments have been
deducted. He does not receive the pensions and other
social benefits of the state, and local arrangements made
by the farms are usually far inferior. He has his private

plot, but private plots are neither prohibited nor uncommon among state employees, and thus need not be affected.

But it would be foolish to think that the collective farms could be changed to state farms, and productivity thereby doubled or tripled, by a mere change of label and accounting systems. We must keep in mind that if the peasant were to get more, the cost would be higher to the state. The state farms have long been the beneficiaries of higher investments by the state, a guarantee to make up deficits, and other subsidies. They have had better management on the whole, and possibly better land as well. Higher productivity has been accompanied by higher wage payments per worker. The state would have to be prepared to meet all these costs, to supply all these resources, and to reduce the labor force and move millions of peasants out of agriculture. All of this is not practical as a sudden transition, although it is undoubtedly aimed at for the future. The collective farms are still needed for one of their collateral functions, that of a reservoir of partly employed peasants, and no decree can strip them down to economic weight faster than the economy can absorb, train, and house the surplus.

▲   ▲   ▲

It will take many years of heavy investment, top-level attention and drive, and changes in policies and organization before the situation of Soviet agriculture is substantially altered. The Soviet goal set forth in the new party program, if achieved, will bring the Russian farms up to the present level of productivity of American agriculture by 1980. But it may be doubted that this will happen. Given the defects of soil and climate alone, Soviet agriculture will probably never be as richly productive as American. But there is no reason why it should not become reasonably adequate to all demands upon it for food and industrial raw materials. The regime has adopted a policy of investment in agriculture which is probably still not adequate, but which is increasing as resources increase. The bent of the Soviet leadership is in favor of "material incentives," and ways will surely be found to tie the income of the peasant more closely to his labor input on the collective, and to reduce more drastically the share of his income owed to his private plot so that he is not drawn so magnetically away from his collective duties.

In the end, the assurance of abundant supplies will depend just as much upon industry as upon agriculture itself. When industry is in a position to supply building materials, roads, trucks, cars, tractors, agricultural machinery, fertilizer, and with all this, large quantities of consumer goods and rebuilt towns for the peasants, the face of Soviet agriculture will begin to change fundamentally. The social revolution, after so long a delay, will in that case create a new countryside as it has created new cities. Only a transformation as profound as this can end the long barren period and assure routine and crisis-free farming. The metamorphosis of the collectives into state farms will probably flow from this. It all depends on whether Soviet industry will prove productive enough to provide for a rural cultural revolution along with everything else it is being asked for.

At the time of Stalin's death, Soviet agriculture was in a true and immediate crisis, and any attempt to continue much longer in the old way would have imperiled the entire economy. Much of the cause for de-Stalinization can be found in this fact, and it is indicative that Khrushchev, who was to find himself at the head of the de-Stalinization drive, was himself chiefly concerned with the problems in agriculture both before and after Stalin's death.

Today, however, the picture is different. We may still use words like "crisis" about Soviet agriculture, but they must be given a far more moderate meaning. The problem now is not imminent shortage of basic crops and the disruption of the whole structure, but rather the providing of a more varied diet, richer in meats, dairy products, vegetables and fruits, the availability of larger surpluses for export, and the accumulation of reserves.

We must remember that the Soviet Union is no longer a predominantly agricultural land. In the twenties, 80 percent or more of the population was rural, and three-quarters to four-fifths of the people lived from farming. Today only half the population is rural, with this percentage shrinking yearly, only about two-fifths of employment is in agriculture or forestry, and—most important —only a fifth or at most a fourth of the total national output is derived from farming. This proportion too is dropping constantly.

This means that the vulnerability of Russia through this particular Achilles' heel is far less than it used to be. The Soviet Union is now irrevocably an industrial country, and we must not forget that many of the most powerful industrial countries of Europe, nations that lorded over the world in their time, could not raise enough food to feed their populations. They had to import it, and their industrial might made this easy. It may seem outlandish to suggest that Russia could be an importer of food, when she has been thought of for so many centuries as the agricultural country of Europe. No doubt this will never happen on any important scale. The point is made, however, as a reminder that Russia's fate now lies with her industry, and to a country with great industrial power many things are possible.

The State
Replaces
the Capitalist:
Complexities of
Planning

Notwithstanding its remarkable growth record, the Soviet economy is far from being a trouble-free system. It is still a crude and unfinished structure, plagued with problems of waste and inefficiency. Despite its super-rational attack on the economic problem by way of central planning and administration, many of its operations exhibit a startling degree of irrationality. A great deal of this unquestionably attaches to the present stage of Soviet development. But since the economy, short of an unattainable ideal frictionless state, will always meet specific problems of operating in a resistant medium, many of the difficulties it now faces must be taken as inherent in the very system of government operation of a giant and complex economy.

Under cover of various circumlocutions and camouflage verbiage, this is in effect recognized by many Soviet and Soviet-bloc economists, and a broad discussion is under way, which some Western economists have been following with great interest. This is part of the rebirth of Soviet economics after Stalin's death, when the discussion of industrial management and economic planning became more frank, and when statististics began to be released to the world in far greater quantity and more scrupulous quality.* Economists have divided into schools which debate reforms and alternatives, within broad limits, without apparent inhibition.

This process was greatly stimulated by the stage the economy entered in the fifties. A new complexity appeared, partly because of massive growth, but chiefly because, in place of the single high-priority sector of the thirties and forties, the economy began an effort to do many big things at once. In addition to the strains put on resources, the multiple effort seriously complicates planning, allocation of materials, and the meshing of the various industries which have a complicated relationship demanding precise proportions and exact delivery schedules.

Where, in the past, deficits in the major goals could be made up at the expense of other parts of the economy, today this is not so readily done. Commitment to the giant new efforts in agriculture, consumer goods, space exploration, arms, foreign aid, and so forth is too public and complete. While these programs—or those considered less important—can and will be pared for the benefit of heavy industry—still the regime's darling—they can no

* An economist for the RAND Corporation said in a paper submitted to Congress in 1959 that "the Soviet authorities have seen fit to release considerably more statistical information about their economy in the last 3 years than they have in the preceding 20."[1]

longer be reduced drastically as in the past. They must even on occasion be unexpectedly increased—as in November, 1962, when a Central Committee meeting increased government investments in agriculture by almost a third over the year before, in a year when investments as a whole were increased only 10 percent.[2]

Granted continued emphasis on capital-goods industries for a long time to come, the Soviet economy has now become a multiple-priority effort. Concentration of resources, always in the past the basic strategy of the planners, becomes an unreliable guide to planning when the rule is *concentrate on many things* in place of the traditional guide, *concentrate on one thing*.

A capitalist economy, basically, solves its problems of this sort through an automatic mechanism. The market provides a combination of planning agency, incentive goad, and impersonal executioner, with a standard of efficiency which may be disputed but must be obeyed by all who function within it. That it is far from perfect as a planner and regulator may be seen from the fact that we have a business cycle, if from no other. Similarly, the standard of efficiency it provides—salability on the market and the profit margin—have obvious social defects. But apart from larger questions, these standards are universal, unambiguous, and unify all aspects of productive efficiency in a single measure—profitability.

A capitalist economy accepts the profit standard as a measure of efficiency, and accepts as "best" those products which survive the test of the market (although monopoly, advertising pressures, and consumer ignorance or debasement of the culture may do much to distort our choices). The coercion of the market is constant and not ordinarily a respecter of persons. It is manipulated in favor of inefficient producers only with great difficulty, and hands down its adverse decisions in the form of punitive levies against profits or outright death sentences without fear or favor.*

Despite appeals and campaigns, Soviet citizens obviously do not perform their work out of a sense of duty to the community, pride in the state, an instinct of workmanship, or ideological stimulus. Of course, such motives are present in Russia as in all societies, perhaps to a larger degree than elsewhere because of the impulse of revolution which still persists, strong feelings of nationalism, the spur of the race with capitalism, and the ideological efforts of the Communist cadre. But these are, even if important, certainly marginal elements. If the Russians are ever to develop a "New Soviet Man" whose labor has become routine and public-spirited, that lies far in the future.

Nor does coercion perform the chief functions of regulation and control, incentive and punishment. Despite widespread use of this in the past, we should be careful not to take our epithets of "slave labor" too literally—now less than before. Concentration camp labor no longer has the place in the economy it had in earlier decades.

The Soviet economy is far more highly unified than anything in the West, but it is not operated on rigid and complete orders from the top down. In a society based on slave labor and overall coercive fiat, problems of planning and motivation would be resolved by force. But such a system, applied to a modern industrial society, could not operate. Its parts would jam and it would soon grind to a halt; alternatively, unbearable pressures would build up

---

* This is an abstract picture of the workings of the market. As all students of economics know, it is greatly modified in the concrete—especially in recent decades. But we are not concerned here with capitalist economy; this abstraction serves us adequately for the purpose of demonstrating the Soviet problems.

and it would explode. In any event, it could not hope to develop any real buoyancy or drive.

Thus Soviet management is not controlled by detailed orders from central bureaus specifying every action, precise product mix, new installations of machinery, hiring and firing, and so on. Rather, it is guided by more elastic norms and general plans, leaving much to the discretion of regional bodies and plant managements. Even in this looser form, however, the system finds it hard to tap the energies and initiatives without which the economy cannot hope to develop full efficiency.

▲   ▲   ▲

The bonus system is the chief incentive mechanism on the managerial level. How significant it is may be seen from the fact that in important sectors of the economy, managerial personnel get an extra 37 percent of their base pay just for fulfilling the output plan; conversely, a near miss can cost from 30 to 50 percent of base pay. For every percentage point of overfulfillment, managers can receive from 2 to 6 percent of base pay. Thus an overfulfillment of 10 or 15 percent could double the pay of a plant manager, while a shortage of only a few percent could halve it.[3]

As bonuses are tied closely to short periods—even to operations in a single month—the Soviet practice of "storming" in the last days of a plan period, followed by exhaustion and slow recovery in the early days of the next period, is naturally common. Other unwise practices, such as poor maintenance of capital equipment in the race for current output, are also encouraged. But these are the least of the difficulties. Worse ones are met in some of the more complex and diversified industries. High bonuses may work smoothly in the production of uniform, homogeneous, easily measured staples of industry, like electric power, pig iron, raw steel, or long production runs of standard items. But when we come to the more variegated products and problems, the matter is of unsuspected complexity.

An indicator of output, such as tonnage, ruble value, number of pieces, may be readily chosen. But insofar as one measure is used, it leads to the neglect of others. A quota set in rubles may lead to a bias in favor of higher priced goods and a neglect of products made of cheaper materials in the rush to meet and exceed the quota. A norm set in tons can lead to heavier designs, or at least to the failure of designers to work out improved lighter ones and get them adopted. Khrushchev himself is authority for the famous example of massive chandeliers, wasteful of metal and tasteless in appearance; he attributed this to the plan which set a quota in weight of finished output. Sheetmetal norms, when stated in tonnage, led to an assortment of thicknesses strangely complete in the heavy range but scarce in light gauges. Revising the plan in terms of goals formulated in square meters brought about a rush to the other extreme. *Krokodil*, the Soviet humor magazine, once carried a cartoon showing a nail factory's total output for the month completed in a single nail; hanging from overhead cranes, it filled the shop from end to end. Russian readers did not have to be told in what terms the plan quota was formulated.

The assortment of products, styles, sizes, colors, and—

most important—spare parts may be skimped mercilessly. Since they are not and cannot be detailed rigorously in the overall directives, they tend in many cases to be crowded to a minimum by plants or regions intent on meeting output goals.

Again, if costs are not also rigorously controlled they will tend to balloon in the process of boosting output. Even if the more obvious cost indicators are subject to verification through the plant budget, hidden uneconomic practices, such as over-heavy foundry casting which increases raw materials costs and imposes more machining time on other plants while making foundry goals easier to attain, may be prevalent. New materials which may add to immediate costs but result in long-term savings may be neglected because of fears that changing may lose valuable production time. The multitude of sins that may be covered by fulfilled output quotas can be seen from some of Khrushchev's remarks at the 22nd Congress:

One must not keep at the helm of economic development managers who are either unfamiliar with or unable to take account of state funds and who see their task only in fulfilling the plan at all costs.

Let us take, for instance, the managers of the Perm Sovnarkhoz [a regional economic council]. It would seem that everything is going on nicely with them. They promptly report on the fulfillment of the task for gross production. But just look at the way they manage economic affairs. Last year every third enterprise of the economic region failed to fulfill the profits plan, as a result of which they fell short in their accumulations by 27 million rubles. The sovnarkhoz paid over 8 million rubles in various fines, lost 7 million rubles through faulty goods, and ended the year with a deficit of 26 million rubles in its turnover funds. You might think, comrades, that the chairman of the sovnarkhoz, Comrade Soldatov, was sub-

jected to severe criticism. Not at all, he was elected to a leading post on the All-Russian Sovnarkhoz.

A relentless war must be declared on waste in the use of raw
material, materials, and electricity. It has been repeatedly
stressed, for instance, that an enormous quantity of metal is
expended uneconomically in our country. In shavings alone
over 4 million tons of metal are expended every year, and a lot
of energy, work time, electricity, and tools are wasted on this.[4]

To go further: Soviet managers have an understandable bias against the adoption of new processes requiring
extensive plant reconstruction, or the introduction of new
machinery, as these changes delay production and inter-
fere with the fulfillment of the plan. This sort of conservatism may be found in any system, but in Russia the
natural elements of shortsightedness are worsened by the
drive for current production, the absence of slack periods,
and the fact that the top personnel of the plant may be
shifted before the new process begins to pay off, as tenure
in managerial jobs tends to be brief. The same is true
of the introduction of new products. "Conservatives,"
Khrushchev told the Congress, "cling to the old like the
devil to a sinner's soul." He cited examples:

Giving successes in technical progress their due, one cannot but see that there are still many unsolved tasks. One must
face facts when new equipment is introduced into production
slowly. For example, take the Likhachev automobile plant in
Moscow. It produces four-ton trucks which were put into production fourteen years ago and have been modernized only
insignificantly. How then can the managers of this factory and
of the Moscow City Sovnarkhoz justify their allegiance to obsolete technology? Why has design work on a new automobile
been going on for six years? After all, the plant has received
much assistance in organizing the production of an improved
car.

The introduction of a new product is sometimes connected with certain expenditures of production, additional trouble, even disappointment. How much simpler and quieter it is to do today what used to be done yesterday, and to do tomorrow what is done today. Unfortunately, there are still managers among us who wish to spend every day in complete quiet.[5]

The attempt to overcome such obstacles as these involves the addition of further standards and quotas for various aspects of production and efficiency. This effort to keep managers advancing simultaneously on all fronts can become a complicated business, involving an entire set of goals, all of which must be met, even while directing chief attention toward enlarging physical quantities of output.

A recent attempt at simplification and consolidation of incentives shifts attention to a cost-reduction plan, which is made the center of the bonus system. Rewards are dependent on the fulfillment and overfulfillment of the plan for lowering costs—but in order to qualify for the graduated bonuses scaled to that effort, the manager must also meet a number of other quotas: for output and delivery of products, for increasing labor productivity, and for introducing new techniques.

Ever more complex and sophisticated incentives are thus a feature of the Soviet economic scheme, as the planners try to find a way to control all aspects of the production picture. It is interesting that discussion has begun among Soviet economists of a method of subsuming all success indicators under a single category, which would correspond to the Western concept of profitability. In itself, used as a tool of accounting and control, the introduction of a profit concept need not alter the functioning of the Soviet economy, or make it more like capitalism in any basic sense. The catch, however, is that in order for profits to have validity as a measure of efficiency, a far less arbitrary price system, subject to market fluctuations, would have to be adopted. If prices are simply set according to costs of production, the profit figure will merely reflect what is already known; if profits are to serve as an independent indicator, they have to be based on new information, which can only be what the product will bring in a competitive market. This would be a novel departure for the Soviet economy. The Russian economists are fully aware of this complication, and attempts to thrash it out are under way at this writing.

Like these incentive problems, the difficulties on the overall-planning level arise from a natural tendency of individuals to protect and advance their interests, in the setting of a society which encourages them to do so by appealing to their acquisitiveness. Setting plan targets involves a contest in pressure from above and concealment from below. Plants, often abetted by district bodies, may understate their production capacity, their stock of machinery, their hoard of materials. They may take care not to exceed their production quotas too much, or it will go harder with them next time. They will take care to perform and report that combination of results which will maximize their returns without prejudicing their position for future gains. In short, as one Western economist has put it, the system "breeds deception, and command elicits simulation." The Soviet citizen on a bonus system, placed in a situation similar to that of the pieceworker in the West or the corporation tax lawyer, does not hesitate to act much the same way. Nor need the behavior be interpreted in an invidious way; each has his eye on his own difficulties and requirements, and the opinions he forms about his plant's capabilities may be quite honest and scrupulous as such things go in this world; the same may be said for his adversary higher up the planning ladder. How we put it makes no real difference; the losses in productive efficiency and the difficulties for planning that result from this form of motivation in the economy are nonetheless real.

Another sort of difficulty, due more to the cumbersome character of the centralized system of materials allocation and the tight supply situation, has also cropped up and has found unofficial solution in some cases. Faced with the possibility that materials deliveries will be slow or short, imperiling the plan, managers tend to over-order and hoard. They employ the famous *tolkachi,* pushers or expediters not provided for by any Soviet table of organization, who arrange informal exchanges or sales outside the allocation plan. In this way some of the rigidities of the supply system are overcome; it may be likened to the manner in which the body grows a network of tiny blood vessels to bypass a constricted or severed artery.

▲   ▲   ▲

Planning investments has become a complicated matter. Up until now, it has not been thought necessary to make interest charges on capital an important feature of the system. Capital investments are not figured at anything like their true function in the economy. This did not matter so much at an earlier stage when the areas of investment and the kinds of equipment to be built were relatively few, priorities were strongly slanted in favor of one or two major fields, and decisions between alternate uses of capital were neither so many nor so delicate that they could not be made by rule of thumb and common sense. Now, however, the planners find plants buying machinery, regions starting projects, central economic bodies undertaking new construction as though the capital invested in these things were available in unlimited supply. There is no general and effective mechanism compelling them to leave the capital for other projects, more important and more quickly productive. This leads to hoarding of machinery which may be needed later on but is not really needed now, and indiscriminate investment without careful enough calculation of the relative merits of alternative projects.

In his Central Committee report to the 22nd Congress, Khrushchev showed the extent of this problem by reporting that there were 100,000 building projects under way in the country at that time, half of them involving the construction of new productive facilities: "With the simultaneous construction of such an enormous number of projects, material and monetary resources are dissipated; many enterprises are commissioned two or three years later than technical facilities permit. Allocated funds are kept frozen for a long time, are not put into economic circulation, are not returned to the state." He recommended a moratorium on new projects for a year, so serious did he consider the situation, in order that available resources be "turned to the speediest completion of the projects already started."[6]

Khrushchev's catalogue of planning aberrations was long and startling, and he capped it by telling the Congress in his summary speech after the discussion that there existed "millions of square meters of ready production areas which were not insured with equipment, and at

the same time hundreds of millions of rubles' worth of
available equipment for which no production areas were
assigned."[7]

▲   ▲   ▲

We have given a picture of some of the various difficulties encountered by the Soviet system in its day-to-day
operations. It cannot be emphasized too strongly, however,
that this is not a full description of how the economy
actually works. Apart from textbook descriptions of the
skeletal framework, the actual operation of the economy
comes to public notice chiefly in attacks on failings.*
To form a picture of the Russian economy in complete
disarray, producing useless junk in mismatched quantities,
would be a great fallacy. One of the Western specialists
most active in uncovering this picture was careful to ap-
pend a caution to a presentation of this material for a
Congressional committee. "There is no doubt," he pointed
out, "that their system works well. If I have chosen to
concentrate on the 'pathology' of Soviet management, the
purpose was not to create the impression of ineffective-
ness, but to illuminate the gap that every economy shows
between the actual and the ideal."[8]

By any reasonable standards, the economy operates
productively, and as we have shown, has great success in

* ". . . there is information on the formal structure, but accounts of
what actually happens appear, if they appear at all, primarily in the context of problems, of frictions, of things that go wrong. . . . This will not,
unfortunately, provide the fully balanced picture of reality which we
ought to have, but such a picture is necessarily elusive, and will remain
so until there is an opportunity for a great deal of 'field work' on Soviet
institutions." (Alec Nove, *The Soviet Economy*, p. 153.)

increasing its efficiency. But the weaknesses will undoubtedly preoccupy Soviet planners and theorists for years to come. They stem from the situation of an economy which has dispensed with the capitalist market but does not possess that communal *élan* to which it aspires as an alternative to the market, and which also needs to develop advanced and sensitive planning techniques suited to a massive and complex economy in which errors have now become far more costly than they were in decades gone by.

Khrushchev made a special point of this in his report on the new party program at the 22nd Congress, pointing out that capital investments in the 1960–1980 period are slated to be two trillion rubles, six times more than was invested in the entire period up to 1960. In this situation every percentage point grows to enormous magnitudes. "On such a scale," he said, "one cannot, literally, make a single step without observing the popular rule: Look before you leap. Here it is absolutely impossible to do without the most precise calculations—what to build, how and where—to obtain the greatest gain with the least possible expenditure." He thus made a spirited plea for "a new and much higher standard of scientific reasoning and economic calculation," using "everything of value . . . that exists in the West, including that which speeds up the turnover of funds and provides a larger return from capital investments."[9]

Soviet economics is today a far cry from the crude dogma that passed for economic theory under Stalin.* The application of advanced mathematical techniques, such as linear programing and input-output analysis, is being pressed. The Soviet Academy of Sciences has set

* "It is not by chance," Leonid F. Ilyichev, a secretary of the Central Committee told the 22nd Congress, "that in the course of several decades no important works on political economy, philosophy, and history were printed."[10]

up a special department for the study of the economic practices of Western countries. The striving for flexibility and a break with the past has led to remarkable debates and expedients. One rubs one's eyes to read a report that the department of econometrics of the Soviet Academy has been closed to economists over twenty-five years of age![11]

As Alec Nove points out, much of the new Soviet economics grapples with a central difficulty of a government-operated economy,[12] which is this: It is impossible for each plant, or regional economic body, or even sectoral economic bodies on the national level, to make decisions that are fully rational and best from the point of view of the all-national outlook and long-term plan. The decisions they make can be guided only by their own knowledge and their own requirements for optimal efficiency, which is not the same thing. Given this fact, there is an inherent bias in the system toward centralization, which renews itself despite all measures of decentralization. But centralization in turn breeds rigidities, top-heaviness, lack of initiative, and the kinds of planning difficulties that have been outlined above.

The alternative to centralized direction is a system in which the state, armed with the profits of the economy, directs investment along the lines of an overall plan while leaving enterprises free to settle their own investment and supply arrangements and to dispose of their output by purchase and sale contracts. Direct negotiations between plants on this order would undoubtedly simplify planning greatly and encourage flexibility, but it would reduce the government's power over the economy and allow it to develop a will of its own. The state would probably lose some control over the tempo of growth.

Experiments along these lines are furthest advanced

in Yugoslavia. But even within the Soviet bloc trials are being made. Czechoslovakia has gone furthest, but Poland and Hungary have also been the setting for important innovations. There may be reason to believe that Soviet planners and economists are using these as experimental pilot projects and that their results will be significant in the decision whether to open efforts along the same lines in Russia itself. Undoubtedly there is fear—at least on the part of one faction—that reduction of control will prove costly. But the more flexible and adventurous feel strongly that anything lost in this way will be more than compensated by the energies released, the simplification of planning procedures, and other advantages of greater plant autonomy. Since their stars appear to be in the ascendant, we can expect continued experimentation and further innovation in the Soviet economy.*

▲ ▲ ▲

As we have pointed out, capitalism offers superb tools for developing the productivity of an economy. Its competitive pressures, especially before monopolistic practices set in, are matchless in their ruthless and impersonal coercive power. They tend to extract the utmost from individuals and production units, and compel the most exact reckoning of costs. The furthest developed capitalist system, that of the United States, has thus worked up a dazzling operational efficiency.

* ". . . a real breakthrough in effectiveness of organization and decision-making one of these days is not an unlikely possibility." (Campbell, *Soviet Economic Power*, p. 188.) This work contains informative discussions of recent Soviet interest in new mathematical methods on pages 99 and 110–113.

The government-operated economy, by contrast, has many shortcomings in this area. Its strong points lie elsewhere. It can make fuller use of resources on a national scale if not at the plant level, without the cyclical ups and downs or prolonged stagnations that afflict the capitalist pattern. It can set its goals and organize resources to reach them, as we have seen in many specific Soviet achievements. The direction and tempo of the economy, within limits, can be decided; this, above all, contrasts with the capitalist countries, which up until now seem only able to await their economic fate with bated breath, instead of being able to decide it—and efforts to change this have thus far met with limited success.

Nevertheless, the disabilities that the Soviet economy labors under are not absolutes. We must take account of the specific stage it functions in. Planning in the context of the feverish industrialization race is harassed by materials shortages, straining of plant facilities to the utmost, and the need to introduce a variety of new products and new industries at an unusually rapid rate.

When basic modernization of the country and its industries has been completed, and production has been routinized along a well-trodden path, many of the problems are bound to be eased. Quota-setting in a situation of regular production of a familiar assortment of articles will take on a less frenetic character. Materials allocation problems will be eased when warehouses, jobbing depots, and the plants themselves can be permitted the luxury of adequate inventories and reserve stocks. Planning becomes easier when it is not a frantic relay race in which factories pass the baton to each other on the run. An economy that has reached a rich plateau, and is able to take full advantage of modern mathematical techniques and electronic data-collecting and -processing systems, may well work much better—at least in these respects—under a nationalized system than it does now. We are thus not necessarily witnessing an outcropping of insoluble troubles that will multiply for decades to come. Some of them may have that character, and may have to be grappled with incessantly. But many of them represent the growing pains of an organism that is developing so rapidly it must keep bursting through any suit of planning clothes the economists fit to it.

We must ask ourselves what this economy will look like and how it will work when it has attained full growth and many of the transitional expedients of the present drop away. This is a real and vital question because while that day may be decades away it is not generations or centuries in the future. In some respects, that next stage will begin to merge into the present one within the years immediately ahead.* The great riddle of the Soviet Union is what sort of affluent society *it* will create; how its structure will operate and what the quality of life will be when production is no longer the chief problem, and instead distribution, popular culture, and the individual, communal, and ethical life of man become the major concerns.

* A sign of the times is the new Soviet attitude toward the expansion of steel production. Until recently steel was king; nothing was allowed to stand in its way, and its expansion was pushed to the utmost. But at the 22nd Congress Khrushchev adopted a tone of easy affluence and pointed out that while steel production could be expanded more than the plan called for, this would not be needed; a 250-million-ton annual capacity would be enough and it could be attained by 1980 at reduced rates of expansion. Within a year after the Congress steel was even being attacked, and Khrushchev spoke of the diversion of funds from what he called "blind" expansion of steel production to a modern chemical industry which would provide lighter and more useful substitutes for steel and which would have broader application to both consumer goods and agriculture. Western analysts have wondered what Russia was going to do with all that steel; the 1980 plan represents a good two-and-a-half times the present American output. The answer may come in a further cutback of the steel goal. Surely the approach of satiation in this product is a significant symptom.

Soviet economy has proved its strength in repeating the achievements of capitalism. But its far greater and more significant tests lie ahead. Can it use its advantages and overcome its defects to the extent of being able to create a new and superior society? If it passes its first test only, its significance will remain what has already been shown— an example to the underdeveloped countries of how to industrialize—but it will offer little future for human progress after industrialization. If, on the other hand, it offers even a partial response to the second test, its example begins to mean something to the most advanced countries of the West, and its significance becomes incalculable.

CHAPTER V

The Consumer: Past, Present, and Future

The Russians paid heavily for industrialization. In the thirties collectivization and the purges brought enormous pressures and hardships. Then the war, immensely destructive of life and property, made the forties a decade of misery. The dictatorial political system and the harsh labor discipline called into being by the rapid pace of industrialization were exacerbated by Stalin's personal tyranny and megalomaniac terror. The apparatus of repression went out of control and whirred for a time at an insane speed not readily attributable to any direct requirements of the government or the society. At the same time, despite the rapid pace of economic advance, the population at large got very little in the way of benefits.

We do not have trustworthy figures of wages or income distribution. Even today, when Soviet statistics are far more reliable and complete, this area is relatively barren for Western researchers. We do have, however, a number of clear indicators that show the trend of living standards in a general way.

First of all, the depressed state of agriculture makes it impossible to believe that living standards could have improved materially during the years from 1928 to Stalin's death. So large a part of family income is spent on meals that the availability of food is the prime factor in the standard of living. We have already seen that food was in no better per capita supply at the end of the period than at the beginning, and there were a number of periods when it was unquestionably worse than it had been at the start of industrialization and collectivization.

We have next the calculations of Soviet national product, and the proportion that went for household consumption over these years. If we follow Bergson's careful accounting, probably the most authoritative to date, we find that the percentage of the country's output used for household consumption fell from perhaps three-quarters in 1928 to around one-half in the late thirties, and then as low as one-third during the war. In the postwar period up until 1952, it remained at only 40 to 45 percent of total output.[1] It rose later and is now somewhat higher; this coincided with the later rise in living standards in the Khrushchev period.

These figures suggest that in the late forties household consumption per capita was no higher than twenty years earlier. Despite the great increase in Soviet national product, the slash in the portion going for households, and the population growth, seem between them to preclude a gain in personal spending. By 1950, however, the enormous expansion was taking effect. Even as little as 45 percent of the national product was now more per person than the three-fourths consumed in 1928. But it could not have been very much more. In that year, total household consumption was probably a little less than 50 percent greater than in 1928, spread among a population almost one-quarter larger.[2]

All of this provides us with only the roughest of guides. It tells us nothing about the distribution of income among high, lower, and lowest paid categories, or between farm and city. It does not take account of the destruction and starvation that accompanied cataclysms like collectivization and the war. And it does not include varieties of deprivation and suffering that cannot be translated into statistics.

We must at this point add an amendment to this bleak picture. There was one respect in which popular living standards rose rapidly. Apart from household consumption, which embraces that part of national income spent by the population on its own personal goods, there is a large category in the Soviet national accounts known as *communal services*. This represents, in effect, the portion of the income of the Soviet citizen which the government spends for him. Every country has it—free public education is the largest example in the West—but in Russia the category is naturally more important than elsewhere.

At the start of the period, in 1928, communal services took 4½ to 5 percent of gross national product. We must keep in mind that even had this percentage remained unchanged, it would have represented an enormous per capita increase in absolute terms, since output was growing so fast. But it did far better than stay the same; by 1937 it had doubled, and has been stabilized since then at 9 or 10 percent of the national product.[3] Enormous sums have thereby been made available for education, pensions, maternity benefits, subsidized holidays, medical care, nursery and boarding schools—and these sums grow from year to year as fast as the burgeoning economy. This is confirmed by innumerable reports from non-Soviet observers, who have found that while the Russians remained throughout the industrialization period badly fed, miserably clothed, and worse housed, in social services they enjoyed an immense advance which brought them, in this respect, up to or above the level of advanced Western nations.

Their personal incomes and spending remained, however, very meager. As to where the funds went, our expectations are readily confirmed by the statistics. Investment increased, in Bergson's calculations, to almost 30 percent of the national product by the end of the forties, probably doubling its percentage of 1928; and armaments spending, amounting to only 2 percent in that year, had increased to 11–13 percent in the postwar period after devouring enormous proportions during the war.[4]

▲   ▲   ▲

The charge that has often been made, that the Soviet people got very little in the form of direct personal benefit out of the industrialization campaign, and suffered much, is thus, apart from the social and educational benefits, certainly accurate. But unless we keep in mind that this rule holds only until the start of the fifties and does not apply to the post-Stalin era, and that it most certainly does not apply to the future, we will make a most serious error. In particular we should be wary of the simple but misleading assumption that the greater the amounts invested in expansion for the future, the poorer the people's living standards. At most, such a rule applies only in the basic period of industrialization, but it has little relevance after the process of accumulation is well under way.

We need only reflect that while this is a rule some tend to apply with great stringency to Russia, few would dream of applying it to the United States. High investment periods in a capitalist economy are normally associated with prosperity, despite the fact that the proportion of the national product available for consumption is lower. The highest United States consumption *rates* on record belong to the years of the depression of the thirties, when investment had fallen almost to zero; yet living standards were cut to the bone because the national output was down to half the predepression levels in the worst years. It is not only the share of the pie that counts, but the size of the whole pie before it is shared.

There is an even more telling comparison: some countries use as little as 5 percent of their output for investment and, having small arms and administrative budgets, consume in the neighborhood of 90 percent of their national product. Yet these countries, characteristically, cannot even maintain their miserable living standards, which are eroded from year to year by a population growth far in excess of economic growth. These are the typical lands of poverty, disease, stultification.

Thus the high level of investment is not in itself the cause of low living standards (although of course living standards in any given year would be higher if less were spent on machines and more on food and clothing). The right way to see the cause of the poverty in the midst of expansion in Russia is to focus on the *rising* proportion of the national output eaten up by investment and armaments. But after these had risen to their more or less stable current levels by the end of the forties and beginning of the fifties, living standards began to rise in rough consonance with the expansion of the entire economy. And we can make the assured forecast that this rapid im-

provement is bound to continue even if the present proportion of the national product going to investment and
arms rises somewhat in the near future. In order to postu-
late a stagnation in Soviet living standards over the next
two decades—as some Western editorial writers have
hastily concluded from the announced Russian plan to
continue growing at almost the same rate throughout this
period—one must commit the most elementary and dis-
astrous errors of economic reasoning. The only way to
reach this conclusion is to believe that investment and its
accompanying nonconsumer categories will swell mon-
strously until they swallow at least four-fifths of Russian
output, double the present two-fifths, which is huge
enough. But if we assume this, we get rates of economic
growth so fabulous they hardly bear thinking about, all
senselessly devoted to building machines that make more
machines.

The fallacy arises from an attempt to think about the
next two decades of Soviet growth in the same terms as
the last three. Actually, in order to grow at the same rate,
the Russians basically need only invest at roughly the
same rate. But if the proportion given to investment (and
arms plus government administration) remains roughly
the same or even rises quite a bit, the amount left over
for Soviet living standards can still rise quickly.

How quick growth will be depends in part on where
investment is concentrated. If it is shifted toward housing
and agriculture, as has been the case for the past few
years, that will slow the rate of growth of the entire
economy slightly while raising the speed of improvement
in living standards. Conversely, if areas with a high return
in product for each unit of capital are the chief field of
concentration, the reverse will be the case. But in any
realistic estimate of the matter, these will be variations

within a generally rapid pace of improvement in living standards.

We may translate this simple economic proposition in the following words: In the period of its great ascent the Soviet Union could do only one thing at a time; it approached its economic task in an exclusivistic way. Everything was thrown into industrialization, and the rest —food, clothing, housing, manufactured goods for the consumer—was taken care of badly or not at all. It is now in a position to do several or all of these things simultaneously, and the big change since Stalin's death is thus due neither to his death in itself, nor to Khrushchev's defeat of Malenkov nor Malenkov's pressure upon Khrushchev, nor any other of the favorite Kremlinological explanations. It accords with the new situation of Soviet society, and it both reflects and stimulates the demand of the Soviet people for relief from their austerity.

This important new capacity of the Soviet economy will dominate the decades of the sixties and seventies, and have immense consequences then and thereafter. In 1960, *Problems of Communism*, a periodical published by the United States Information Agency, printed a symposium initiated by Alec Nove in an article called "Toward a 'Communist Welfare State'?" Two of the contributors made specific explanations of the point we have been discussing, and in view of the signal importance of the matter, their remarks are worth quoting.[5]

Bertrand de Jouvenel, the noted French economist, wrote:

Increasing the shares of investment and government consumption in national production obviously narrows the share of private consumption. But if—as economists universally agree— the allocation of a large share to investment fosters a high rate of increase in over-all output, then it is a simple matter of arithmetic to show that output for consumption, in absolute terms, will also rise rapidly, even though as a proportion of the total product it may continue to decline. . . .

. . . The volume of consumer goods turned out by Soviet industry has increased considerably. It is claimed that in 1958 the index for purchases of textile products stood at 183 (1940 = 100) for workers' families, and at 204 for the families of collective farmers; and that the corresponding index figures for purchases of leather footwear were 201 and 217 respectively. These figures do not strike me as implausible. Indeed, it would be hard to imagine any countervailing factors powerful enough to prevent a build-up of productive capacity such as has been taking place in the U. S. S. R. from resulting in a considerably increased output of industrial consumer goods.

The same point is even more sharply made by Peter Wiles, head of the department of economics at Brandeis University, who, writing about the "Soviet obsession with a more rapid rate of growth for heavy industry," remarks:

Maximum consumer satisfaction at any moment of time would require a relaxation here also. But it is far from clear that the Western policy in this regard is right, and the Soviet wrong, if we are thinking of consumer satisfaction not merely now but in the future. In the long run, if Soviet consumption continues to grow at anything like its present rate, it will exceed the American rate; hence it is not clear why this policy should be altered or that it is, in any permanent sense, a defect of the Soviet system.

An attempt is made by Bergson to work this proposition out with figures. He points out that "with total output growing as it now is at more than 7.0 percent yearly, and with the population growing at but 1.8 percent yearly, the government is able to increase the rate of investment and yet at the same time to raise not only aggregate but per capita consumption." Even if the physical volume of capital investment were boosted from year to year at a rate of 10 percent, well above the 7 percent overall growth, he points out, this would still leave the possibility of a rate of increase in consumption of 2.8 percent per person per year, which is unusually rapid. He calculates that per capita consumption has been rising by 6 or 7 percent a year during the fifties. "Under Stalin," he concludes, "the Russian people paid heavily for an acceleration in the rate of growth of total output. Now that a high tempo has been achieved there should be no need for them to pay any comparable price in order to maintain the tempo of increase under Stalin's successors."[6]

▲   ▲   ▲

"For forty years," a Russian recently told a British visitor, "we have been asked to work for the future, for posterity, for our grandchildren, and now at last we are being asked to work for something which we can have in our hands *now*."[7] Khrushchev has found this theme quite naturally to his liking, and developed it with variations at the 22nd Congress. "Will the mobilization of such vast means," he asked, "not involve difficulties and sacrifices, even as during the period of industrialization?" And he replied:

We have every reason to answer this question in the negative, in the first place, because our country has created a powerful industry. The role of heavy industry in the growth of national well-being, as well as in the solution of the problem of accumulation is now manifested in a new way. It is known that heavy industry includes two types of enterprises: First, those which produce production means for enterprises which in turn produce means of production; second, enterprises which produce means of production for enterprises of the light and food industries, for agriculture, for housing construction, and everyday cultural services for the people.

When our heavy industry was only just being created we were forced to direct accumulations primarily to enterprises of the first type and restrict investments in the second group of enterprises. Now we have the opportunity to substantially increase capital investments in enterprises of the second type, which will accelerate the rate of growth of popular consumption. . . .

In the next twenty years production by all branches of industry producing consumer goods is to increase about five times.[8]

In the thirties, as Khrushchev pointed out, the rate of increase of production of capital goods was fully 70 percent higher than the rate of increase of consumer goods. In the plans for the next twenty years the former is to grow at a rate only 20 percent faster than the latter. This is so sharp a break from Soviet tradition that, despite the gap between them, Khrushchev says there is to be an "approximation" between the two; they are now at least in the same general class. Capital goods will multiply by 7 times while consumer goods will multiply by 5, according to the plan.

In the brief six-year period between the 20th and 22nd Congresses, state investments, totaling 156 billion rubles, added up to more than in the preceding Soviet period of three decades.[9] Yet this took place at a time when expenditures on living standards were, as we have seen, mounting rapidly, when the demands of the armed forces were rising faster, when agriculture was getting heavy sums, and when new fields like foreign aid and space exploration were making heavy inroads on resources. All of this contributes to our new picture of a Soviet economy able to make powerful thrusts in a number of fields at once.

With all this, a Hofstra College economist who specializes in Soviet living standards has estimated the potential for per capita increase now at about 5 percent annually. Since the recent trend has been for farm incomes to mount faster, he says, "urban consumption levels may be rising by slightly less than 5 percent annually."[10] When we consider that this is at least double and more likely triple the best American per capita gains in consumption in recent decades, we can get something of an idea of what is in the offing for the Russian consumer. Although he starts from a miserably low level, he is moving up very quickly indeed. And no Soviet regime will be able to bring this to a halt. In a typically forthright mood, Khrushchev told the delegates to the 21st Congress: "We should recognize that the further we move ahead . . . the more assertive and uncompromising will be the working people's attitude toward hardships. Why? Because people want to see the successes in economic development in the stores and in their shopping bags."[11]

▲   ▲   ▲

For many years the possibilities of the Soviet system for raising popular living standards were open to serious doubt. From its origins in the European socialist movement and from its entire initial orientation, we know that Bolshevism wanted to raise them, and as a matter of fact undertook industrialization with that end in view. But the long stagnation of living standards or their absolute decline, and the changes in the outlook of the regime, led many to maintain that this had altered. Alexander Eckstein argued persuasively as recently as 1955 that the Stalinist solution to the dilemma of how to industrialize not only cut the Gordian knot with a sword of compulsion, but at the same time lost sight of the original goal. The industrialization that was originally desired for purposes of a welfare economy became, he said, "a power-oriented program of economic development." The object became not welfare but the strength of the state.[12]

This argument may be right or wrong—it is hard to settle, dealing as it does with an intangible like "the purpose of the state" or a psychological complexity like the motives of the leaders—but right or wrong it is certainly incomplete, and for this reason we find much empirical evidence piling up against it. If it is now the intention of the Soviet leaders to restrict consumption to the barest minimum in order to leave all resources free for the pursuit of power, they have certainly gone about it in a peculiar way in the last decade. Through innumerable public pronouncements, party and government resolutions, and now the vast long-term program of the party, they have stimulated a prodigious revolution of rising expectations. They have inaugurated production programs that have already considerably raised consumption, and—most important— they have committed themselves irrevocably to promises that clash sharply with any notions of restricting consumption. This may all arise from pressure by the people, but the regime has at very least catered to it; actually, the regime has stimulated it.

It may be objected that popular welfare is itself an element of power in the reckoning of the leaders of the

Soviet state, that it is essential for their purposes to raise living standards at least to the level of Western Europe right away, and that they will win an enormous power victory if they succeed in overtaking American living standards. This too is true: welfare becomes a means of power, and may best be pursued by industrial development, which is also the basic path to power of other sorts.

All of this is surely correct, but if we try to explain away Soviet welfare moves by this argument, we raise thought-provoking implications. We have, by this interpretation, simply destroyed the antagonism between power and welfare. Popular welfare is unquestionably a major element in the power of any state, including the nations of the West.

We may put an invidious interpretation on the Soviet leaders' motivations, but we gain nothing thereby, either analytically or propagandistically, and probably will only wind up by exasperating the uncommitted peoples, who see no reason to believe that Khrushchev begrudges his people the bread they put in their mouths any more than does Kennedy. History may not be able to detect the difference between an expansion of power for the sake of welfare and an expansion of welfare for the sake of power. In any case these motivations may be impossible to untangle in the complexities of individual and social psychology, and they add little to an objective interpretation.

The growth of the welfare of the Russian people—at least as reckoned only in material living standards—is likely to be great in the years ahead, and it will prove fruitless to concoct theories that either deny this or give it an evil twist. The error would be just as egregious as that committed by the Russians in refusing to recognize the rise in Western living standards.

What is more to the point is the difference in concepts

of welfare embodied in the two societies and propagated by the two sets of leaders, East and West. The use of resources for popular consumption will be sharply different. In capitalist society the ideal embraces primarily privacy, fragmentation, the individual pursuit of happiness. The Soviet ideal is communal, social rather than private, and requires in its present form a tutelary relation between people and state.

These divergent paths are not merely ideals; each is enforced by and stems from a powerful economic mechanism that is an integral part of the society. As the Soviet Union gathers resources with which it may apply its conception of the public good on a broadening scale, it will contrast ever more sharply with the industrial society of the West, which it has hitherto been so intent on emulating.

CHAPTER VI

The Quality
of Life:
Communal Services

Speaking on October 20, 1961, to the 22nd Congress of the Soviet Communist Party, Anastas I. Mikoyan, probably the most authoritative voice of the era next to Khrushchev himself, offered a clear and coherent exposition of the current theory of what is called "the transition to communism."[1] He approached the subject by way of a polemic against Stalin's last work, *Economic Problems of Socialism in the U. S. S. R.*[2] and against the decisions of the 19th Congress, held in October, 1952, just before Stalin's death.

The then dominant idea, Mikoyan explained, was that communism would be brought into being chiefly by two changes: the constant growth of production to the point where real wages could be at least doubled from the 1952 level; and the abolition of collective farm property and remnants of private trade, with their replacement by state farms and the direct exchange of goods between farm and city. This, according to Mikoyan, was a "vulgarly simplified concept." He attacked both propositions.

In the first place, he said, the prejudice against collective farms misconstrued their role in the transition to communism. While it is true that there will be only one form, communal property, he argued, state farms are not in themselves closer to this than collectives. They suit different purposes under differing conditions, but both promote "the movement of our society to communism." Both can aid in the "building of the material and technical basis of communism," and in "creating the one and only form of communist property."

While Mikoyan's view is also open to criticism as a crude simplification, it is an important modification of traditional doctrine, which put collective farms lower on the scale of social change than state farms. It projects a direct evolution of both kinds of farms to a higher form, instead of the necessity for the collectives to first pass through the state-farm stage. From a practical point of view it portends the continuation and strengthening of the collective farms, with their mixture of private and public enterprise, for a long time to come, as we have already argued in our discussion of Soviet agriculture.

Mikoyan's second point, however, is far more interesting and important. He attacked the idea that communism involves only the raising of standards of living and culture. The magic minimum repeatedly cited at the 19th Congress was a "doubling" of wages. But by 1965, Mikoyan said, real wages would already be two and a third times their 1950 level. "And yet we cannot in any way state that this will insure the transition to communism." Along with the rise in living standards, the form of distribution is also decisive, and in this respect the Stalinist perspective was the very opposite of what it should have been:

A concept of this sort suggested a wrong direction for future policy in the field of distribution. It was interpreted as the transformation of wages into the only form of distribution. It was proposed that everything be paid for; it was proposed to increase rents, as Molotov demanded; to charge for industrial protective clothing; to increase fares and tariffs for communal services, decrease the grant fund, and introduce education on a paid basis. In a word, they were advocating the curtailment of public consumer funds, and rejecting their growing role in the transition to communism.[3]

We have in Mikoyan's speech a graphic illustration of the ambivalence of the Khrushchev Interregnum as it was described by Deutscher in his brilliant lectures in Canada in 1959.[4] The scrapping of Stalinist dogma facilitates moves toward more material incentives and more imitation of Western techniques in planning. It also delineates an opposite tendency, to institute anticipatory forms of socialized distribution, in the sharpest possible break with Western capitalism. These divergent paths stem from the possibilities and limitations of the society. In the area of production, years or decades of effort remain before the economy can catch up with capitalism. In the field of distribution, the industrialization that has already been accomplished is providing big resources for consumption, and the aim is to make a start at distributing them in a revolutionary way.

Mikoyan continued:

We cannot advance toward communism adhering to the distribution of communal products through wages alone. For the question is one of creating a communist way of life. In the new program it is shown that in the period of the general long-term prospects, satisfaction of the citizens' needs will be realized both through wages, the main form of distribution, and through rapidly growing public consumer funds, which should be so directed that they will not oppose the principle of material incentive and will assist the solution of a series of major problems in the building of communism.

According to calculations, by the end of the 20-year period both forms will occupy an approximately equal position in the system of distribution, and thereafter the public form of consumption will begin to prevail. Such a policy enables correct combination of socialist distribution in accordance with labor and the policy of liquidation of economic inequality, which so far still continues to remain among us.[5]

Although this thought is linked by the Soviet rulers to the "transition to communism," a prospect which, we shall see later, is very remote, it embodies measures which are neither visionary nor utopian. It is a practical proposition, which we may expect to see in ever greater measure in the coming decades. Taken by itself, it will not provide the superior quality of life that the Soviets say they are aiming for; other developments—in culture, politics, ethics—are more important for that. But even considered separately from these, it foretells quite concretely a vast area of Soviet life which will be very different from that of the West.

The idea of public consumption funds is by now very familiar in capitalist countries. With the rise of welfare spending, we have grown accustomed to a new type of item in the national budget—spending for consumption done by the government instead of the individual. Proponents call this a trend toward the community doing what individuals cannot do well, or perhaps even at all, for themselves. Antagonists say the government is giving the people what it thinks they ought to have, instead of letting them keep the cash and decide for themselves. However described, this trend has already attained an importance in Russia which far exceeds anything similar in the West. It will be recalled that about one-tenth of Soviet gross national product is applied to public consumption funds. A brief review of the nature and extent of these spending programs already in operation is essential at this point. For this purpose we shall follow an excellent outline of the subject drawn up by a Western economist not long ago.[6]

▲   ▲   ▲

As in the Western countries, there exists in Russia a system of free public education. Unlike most Western systems, however, this one extends through the college and university level, where free tuition is supplemented by free books and, most striking, stipends to pay living expenses are awarded to students who maintain scholastic minimums, as most do. Despite the guarantee of the Soviet Constitution of 1936 that all education would be free, Stalin in 1940 imposed charges in the top three grades of secondary school and in the colleges, but these were all abolished in 1956. Soviet school facilities are overcrowded and some are antiquated, but a large building program is under way. The pupil-teacher ratio is far more favorable than in many other countries; in the mid-fifties it was only 16.6 pupils per teacher as against a United States figure of 26.9 and a United Kingdom figure of 25.8.

Again, like Britain and some other countries in the West, Russia has a system of socialized medicine. Medical care is free, although like education it is hampered by shortages of buildings, equipment, and drugs; but the number of doctors per thousand population is much

higher than in Britain, and somewhat higher than in the
United States, West Germany, and other Western countries.* Total budget allocations for health, education, social security, social insurance, and maternity assistance in
1959 was precisely double the figure in 1950, roughly in
keeping with the growth of the economy.

Sickness benefits are paid to trade-union members on
a scale ranging from 50 percent of earnings for those with
less than three years service to 90 percent for those with
more than twelve. This is subject to a minimum, and the
lowest-paid workers receive close to their full wage when
ill. Nonmembers of unions get half of these amounts (subject to the same minimum), but the vast majority of those
eligible are members—for this reason alone, coercion
apart. Paid maternity leave, which before 1938 was
granted for a total of 112 days before and after confine-
ment, was reduced in that year to 70 days, but in 1956
restored to its former length.

Pre-1956 old-age and permanent-disability pensions
used to pay a maximum of 200 (old) rubles a month, a
figure that had been set a quarter-century earlier and was
long out of date, but in 1956 this was raised to 300 rubles
for those qualifying by length of service, and a new scale
of payments gave the average worker perhaps slightly less
than two-thirds his pay, although he is no longer allowed to continue working and draw his full pension; if he
does, he will normally get only 150 rubles pension a
month. Vacations vary from two weeks for the largest
group of workers (almost half) up to four or even more
for the rest, with the more generous vacation provisions

* It is typical of the Soviet economic situation that buildings and
equipment are in short supply, while manpower is plentiful. As we see,
this affects education and medical care too—although the training of so
much professional manpower is impressive.

reserved for workers in arduous and unhealthful occupations.

This brief review serves to indicate the nature and extent of present welfare spending, although it does not include such things as inexpensive books, partially subsidized housing and resort vacations, relatively low-cost cultural and theatrical events, and an astonishing number of libraries. Until approximately 1950, this was the only field in which the Soviet working people secured tangible benefits from their heavy labors, and this area of rewards continues to expand rapidly. Summarizing the trend, an American economist wrote recently: "Generally speaking, the area of communal consumption—principally the free health and educational services, as well as the partially subsidized consumption of housing—seems to be expanding at a faster rate than the sector producing goods and services with price tags that more or less ration their supply. Direct taxes are being reduced and transfer payments (pensions and grants) are being liberalized. As a consequence, ordinary measures of real wage changes taking account of only the movements in price and money wage levels tend to understate the real improvement in Soviet levels of living."[7]

▲   ▲   ▲

It should be noted that not all of the benefits cited in the foregoing review fall into the communal-spending category in the full sense. Sickness benefits and pensions, for example, or even educational stipends on which college students support themselves, redistribute to specific individuals money gathered by general levies on the population. In Western economies, we call these simply "transfer payments," and while they have an effect on the distribution of income, their use remains in the hands of individual and household consumer units. True communal spending, by contrast, is better exemplified by education itself, or medical care, sanitation services, all goods and services distributed free; their hallmark is that the government, not the individual, does the spending and chooses the commodity or service.

The projections for this form of expenditure in the new program adopted at the 22nd Congress are ambitious. The key paragraph says: "At the same time, as the country advances towards communism, personal needs will be increasingly met out of public consumption funds, whose rate of growth will exceed the rate of growth of payments for labor."[8] As we have seen from Mikoyan's remarks, the program provides that within twenty years all spending for consumption will be divided half and half—fifty percent for personal consumption expenditures, and fifty percent for communal. Since the present ratio is something like five to one in favor of private spending, the program's statement that the rate of growth of the latter "will exceed the rate of growth of payments for labor" is an understatement. If this plan is carried through, the entire spending structure will undergo a radical transformation.

Some of the projects are simply extensions of present programs. Rents, for example, are now very low, ranging from about 2 to 5 or 6 percent of income, and the charge for utilities is nominal. During the seventies these are to be abolished altogether. The minimum length of annual paid holidays is to be increased to three weeks, and later to one month. The national vacation and social insurance programs are to be extended to the collective farms. Pres-

ent medical care services are to be enlarged by the provision of free drugs and free sanitarium treatment.

But with something like restaurant meals, we come to
a new type of provision. It is planned to make a transition
in the second decade of the twenty-year period to free
midday meals in schools, factories, and collective farms.
Public catering in canteens and restaurants is to be encouraged as a matter of social policy: "Price reductions in
public catering will keep ahead of price reductions for
foodstuffs in the shops." The quality of food and service
"must be radically improved, so that meals at public catering establishments should be tasty and nourishing and
should cost the family less than meals cooked at home."
Through such changes and price pressures, the program
hopes that public catering will "take precedence over
home cooking within 10–15 years."[9]

Even more sweeping is the educational plan, which is
a program to take over a large part of the costs of raising
children—and with costs, of course, partial control. There
are to be free hot meals at school, including extended
school hours and dinners as well as lunches; the free provision of school uniforms and educational aids; and many
more kindergartens, nurseries, playgrounds, camps, all
providing full-time care without charge. The next step
beyond this is the complete raising of children in boarding
schools through the basic school years.[10] Introduced in
1956, these schools now have about 600,000 students, many
from broken or impoverished homes or from other problem situations. It is planned to enlarge this enrollment to
two and one-half million by 1965, and thereafter to try
to make a place available for every child whose parents
wish him educated in a boarding school.

Summarizing these plans, Khrushchev told the 22nd
Congress: "So, while the main part of the expenses for

maintenance of children is now borne by the working people themselves, by the end of the next twenty years, approximately 75–80 percent of the expenses for the maintenance and education of children will be borne by society."[11] Westerners hear this with mixed feelings, and undoubtedly want to know what sort of society it will be that will pay the piper and call the tune.

To the above, the program adds a number of other things, including free public transportation; steady reduction of charges for and partially free use of holiday homes, boarding houses, and tourist camps; expansion of other grants, like those to unmarried mothers.[12]

▲　　　▲　　　▲

The repeated use of the word "free" in connection with public consumer expenditures should not be taken literally. In the West also we speak of free highways, education, street-cleaning services, libraries, but everybody realizes that nothing produced by human effort is free; it is all a matter of shifting costs. The government provides these services only by retaining part of the social income; a philanthropist provides them by parting with some of his wealth; a community levies a special assessment on its members.

Thus there can be in such a program no magical bestowal of largesse. Some "free" economic gains can be achieved by elimination of waste and duplication through large-scale programs. Several hundred restaurant-style meals might be cheaper than if prepared individually in home kitchens, if the labor of the housewife is figured into the costs. A free mass-transportation system would not be free to society, but it might be slightly less expensive, if only by the amount required to police it against nonpaying riders, and collect, handle, and reckon fare income. Such gains might turn out to be of some significance, but could hardly be decisive. Thus the Russians will still be paying for what they get.

But if we leap from this fact to the conclusion that the whole thing is nothing but a small change in form, and alters nothing essential, we will be making a big mistake. There are great immediate consequences in such a change, and great potentialities for transforming the entire social fabric. It is another mode of using the economic and social power of the Soviet state for a new sort of revolution, not merely a continuation of the old one of industrialization. It is fraught with vast possibilities for good and for evil. The one thing that it is not is just "the same old thing in different form," as some have hastened to conclude.

The Russians argue for it in a number of ways, which are worth listing, as they give us an idea of the aims being set for the society:

1. Every free distribution, since it separates access to the commodity or service from the ability to pay, is an equalitarian step. Given enough such steps, and a reduction in income inequities, and you stand on the threshold of an equalitarian society—"to each according to his needs."

2. Certain kinds of household consumption, like home cooking and laundry, bear inequitably *within the family*. Freeing the woman of these chores will enable her to take her place as a full member of society, on a par with the man.

3. Waste, inefficiency, and petty duplication being

eliminated, better services become possible—for example, more varied, scientific, and nutritious menus.

4. Community life and social spiritedness are encouraged, to the detriment of "selfish individualism."

5. A communist form of life, in which the basic requirements of life and culture are taken for granted by every member of society without regard to the specific work-contribution he makes—which is also taken for granted as his best effort—is gradually developed through this mode of distribution along with other improvements in society and culture. In this way, a communist form of life can grow organically, and need not be "imposed."

We can return later to a discussion of this perspective, which in its larger implications is—no matter what the Russians may claim—a very distant possibility, and take the matter up in a much more immediate way by raising here another contrast with the West.

An uneasy feeling has developed in the United States and other places in recent years that the West faces a problem of social balance that is becoming more acute with each passing year.* Capitalism tends to develop private expenditure, it is said, at an unchecked rate, while curtailing public service expenditures stringently. While automobiles, household appliances, television, food, clothing, and the like are produced on a lavish and impressive scale, the cities grow dirtier and the slum blight spreads, education and medical care fall behind needs, shortages imperil every area of public administration. This has reached the point where even the enjoyment of private luxuries is nullified by public neglect. Cars proliferate amazingly, but the avenues are clogged and the countryside ever less attractive. Television is in almost every home, but it is

* To date, the most persuasive and popular exposition of this theme is John Kenneth Galbraith's *The Affluent Society,* Boston, 1958.

sacrificed to goods-peddlers, and a mass audience increasingly ill-equipped for its discriminating use is thus subjected to cultural exploitation. "This contrast of public squalor and private opulence, this failure of emphasis in our economy, this preoccupation with private consumption against public consumption," is the description given by Adlai Stevenson.[13]

This is not the place to undertake a critique of Western society, but it is important to call attention to the problem of social imbalance because, from our entire preceding discussion, it is clear that Russian industrial society is taking a different line. We should not be deceived by recent manifestations of a desire on the part of the Russian people for more household appliances, cars, television sets, and Parker 51 pens. This pressure exists, and the government will satisfy it—within limits. But the bias of the system is in the other direction, and the regime has decisive tools in its hands for shaping the society in accord with that bias.

We cannot know what sort of country will emerge—because its shape depends on many other things as well, and because projections, no matter how rigorous or imaginative, have only a limited validity. Still, we can form conjectures about some aspects.

The impact on the home will undoubtedly be great. This will not tend to be a home-centered society, and gracious living will not be conceived chiefly in terms of personal possessions and home entertainment. We have seen something of the same trend in the West, but in the Soviet Union this natural tendency of industrial society will be intensified. The very nature of apartment construction now going on—the designs, the space limitations—already make this inevitable, and the system of communal services will reinforce it. The home ceases to be the indispensable center for meals and other family functions. Just what it becomes in place of this, apart from a bedroom, is not really clear, and depends on the evolution of the family as an institution under Soviet conditions of feminine employment on a nearly equal basis with men. The family in Russia today is apparently still a very strong unit. But community institutions will undoubtedly expand greatly in importance as centers of social life, entertainment, and providers of former household services.

At the same time, Soviet society will have the power to prevent the debasement of culture by what we may call the lowest-common-denominator effect of a commercial society—but only have the power; it is by no means yet assured that this will be accomplished. The profit standard, we noted earlier, has the advantage of reducing all indicators to a single measure, and thus providing a simplified standard of success in economic life. Now we must face the fact that this standard may be *too* simplified. It has an irresistible and ubiquitous force that reduces mass culture, entertainment, and the amenities to the lowest common denominator by giving great advantages to the goods and services of widest sale—to the detriment of all other standards. As many have noted, this has led to a dominion of the so-called teen-age market over our mass cultural life—the rule of the most avid, energetic, unified, and broadest category of seekers after diversion—and also of course the least mature.

A distribution system that is insulated against this pressure can take various forms. In place of the blind forces of the market we have the possibility of political and social voluntarism. The community can shape the culture directly. Or it can be shaped by appointed arbiters of taste chosen for their political reliability. Or it can work out a system for permitting diversity while preventing debasement. How it will be done depends upon the total evolution of the society. In Russia thus far it has had some good points and many bad ones. Looking at the country, many will be tempted to bear the ills they have rather than fly to others they know not of. Much clearly depends on the chances of combining the existing economic and social leverage with a democratic structure and a mature and thoughtful citizenry.

In approaching these problems, the present Soviet rulers bring with them a number of weighty biases, of which we need mention only the most obvious. During the long industrialization drive they developed ingrained habits of retaining in their own hands as much control over the social product as possible. Now that so much more is going to be available for discretionary spending, the natural bent of the Soviet rulers is to continue in the same fashion. The habits of command, paternalism, and the well-developed conviction that they know best what is good for the people, are bound to be carried over into the new situation.

In view of this, the correction of the Western imbalance may be accomplished at the price of tipping the scale in the other direction. Social expenditures can be expanded beyond their proper due, taking away from individuals things that might better be left to them. In other cases we may expect to see an excessively centralized control over the expenditure of communal funds, and an attempt to dictate forms of life rather than let them grow out of the popular will, or out of an education toward the highest standards. We may well be suspicious of the standards set by an unchecked public power, in the hands of leaders with the limited social horizon, the arbitrary habits of rule, and the special biases bred in the years of the hard ascent.

We thus confront an important contradiction in Soviet society: put most simply, the means to a good life will be available to it, and some of the institutions will be favorable to the conscious shaping of the culture along superior lines; but the rulers, structure, habits, and outlook bred by the hard struggle to get to this advantageous point stand in the way of the balanced and harmonious development of a good society. This contradiction is the most important single social feature of the Soviet Union today, and will no doubt continue to be so in the coming decades.

CHAPTER VII

Equality,
Inequality, and
Social Classes

A generation ago, R. H. Tawney advocated the expansion of social expenditures—giving them the name "communal provision"—as the chief method of redistributing wealth and fighting inequality in Great Britain.[1] No reader of his trenchant polemical analysis can doubt the equalitarian effect of expanding communal services, whether in Britain in the thirties, or in Soviet Russia today.

The effect naturally varies with the nature of the service that is shifted over to free distribution. In the case of mass urban transportation, given the small size of the usual fare, the equalitarian effect is not great when it is offered free to all, except for the very lowest-paid of the population. In the cases of free midday meals, free medical care, free education and boarding schools, the impact is progressively greater, even to the point of giving entire sections of the population access to social advantages they could not possibly have had otherwise.

Some of these effects are more or less automatic. The

free use of transportation facilities and other universal conveniences exemplifies this. But where the facilities are more limited and still must be rationed in some way, or where they are unequal in quality, things are by no means so automatic.

Housing is a good example. Soviet rents are so nominal that the percentage they ordinarily take out of a worker's income is not too different from that taken from the pay of a highly paid functionary, and there is no reason why the one should not be able to pay for as good an apartment as the other. This has led to a considerable amount of mixing of professions and trades in the housing developments, and it will be interesting to see whether this trend expands and what its results are for the entire social picture. But in conditions of a housing shortage, special favors may go to the privileged strata. High officials, writers, and other favored persons are alloted extra space.[2] Some co-operatives have been built where floor space is not rationed according to size of family, and purchasing an apartment in one of these is expensive; here the big income disparities take effect. The government is now reportedly discouraging this sort of building.*

The same problem applies to higher education. The Soviet system promises to all equal opportunity for higher education, and backs that promise by paying the bill. But in the nature of any modern society at this stage of human history, equal opportunity does not mean that all will get higher education, but simply that while a percentage will get it, all will have an equal chance to be among that

---

* At a recent chess match between two Soviet grand masters in Moscow attended by a crowd of 15,000 (ballet dancers represented the pieces on a huge chessboard so that the audience could follow the moves), a troupe of singers almost broke up the show with a ditty about government distribution of newly built apartments: "Kings get five-room apartments," they sang. "Knights get single rooms, and pawns get nothing at all." The crowd applauded long and lustily.[3]

group. The use of influence deriving from income and prestige distorts this picture as well. The Soviet press has been full of complaints that influence has been used by prominent people on behalf of their children. One of the more popular young playwrights has written a play bitterly attacking the practice.[4] Ghostwriting rings for supplying theses, and even examination stand-ins to help well-paying applicants make the required grades, have been flushed out in some major cities.[5] These practices undoubtedly affect only a minor segment. But a larger problem exists. We know in the West the extent to which scholastic averages are affected by the family and background of the child whose home surroundings may from an early age bring him into contact with books, conversation of a certain sort, and other advantages that affect his capacity for absorbing and verbalizing concepts. In Russia today, where education is all important, this may in effect be a minor way of passing on an inheritance to children in place of more tangible accumulations.

Equality is thus bound up not only with consumption patterns, but with the entire social fabric. Unless Soviet society develops a distinctive structure, and an exceptionally rapid expansion of higher education, it will, as other countries, tend toward a self-perpetuating elite. We must at this point return to certain basic considerations about Soviet society stemming from the mode of industrialization that will help us to see this problem.

In the industrialization of the West, the capitalists played the decisive role. While we have hitherto spoken of the "profit motive" or the "pressures of the market" as though these were disembodied forces, all social abstractions have to operate through human beings. The drive and exertions of those who owned personal capital and sought to expand it furnished the motive power for the social and economic organization. Such persons assembled labor armies, set great stores of raw materials in motion, decided on construction projects and saw that they were carried out, overcame opposition, and brought into play the powers of government to aid and protect their enterprises. They decided and others adjusted; they dictated and others obeyed; they paid and others served.

The Soviet Union, similarly, has its social differentiation and hierarchy of command. The "state" took the place of "capitalism" but the one is no more a sheer abstraction than is the other. Both have their captains of industry, generals of the army, and virtuosos of organization. The capitalization of Russia without capitalists thus brought into being a new ruling stratum. The original revolutionary grouping, under the influence of an outlook that required industrialization and modernization, set the process in motion, recruiting specialists and technicians of the old regime or from abroad and giving them a privileged status without which they would not work. Then, in the course of time, a new and numerous body of managers, professionals, and bureaucrats was created.

Formally, these layers at the top of the social pyramid remained on a footing identical with that of the other employees of the state and state enterprises, claiming no rights of ownership, although complete control was in their hands. Privileged in their living conditions, and privileged to command, they enjoyed the powers of decision and compulsion, and wielded them over other men as ruthlessly as such powers have ever been used.

The early revolutionary ideal, of course, had been intensely equalitarian, and elements of that remained in various forms throughout the worst years. But as the tempo of industrialization quickened and the ruling hierarchy grew apace, its boldness increased and it arrogated to itself ever greater privileges. Stalin's rise to power hastened this, as he supplied these strata with a rationale and a protector. Income differences widened, concentration of authority increased, and a new emphasis on rank, decorations, insignia, and deference to all these, made an appearance, not only in the army but in civilian life as well. Reaching a peak in the late thirties, these trends invaded all aspects of Soviet life. Even within the working population, the piecework system, honors and badges, and wide income disparities were used as incentives and had the effect of recruiting a favored stratum.

▲   ▲   ▲

As in the case of so many other issues, the Khrushchev regime confronts social differentiation and inequality with an ambivalent attitude. On the one hand, the regime is intimately bound up with the existing structure of privilege; it also needs the policy of income disparity to continue to drive the economic machinery. On the other hand, in its efforts to rally support and enthusiasm, and under the pressure of a now-reviving popular egalitarianism, it has refurbished the revolutionary goal of a classless society, and is seeking with characteristic vigor to cut down the worst excesses of the old regime. Thus, although the system of privilege and command remains, not since Stalin's famous speech in 1931 denouncing equalitarianism as a heresy has there been so strong a current running against the inequities of Soviet life. This has resulted in a series of important measures.

Since 1955 the use of massive price cuts to pass on

gains in production to the consumer appears to have declined in importance. Instead, a policy of selective corrections of income and wage inequities has been followed. The statutory minimum wage was raised in 1957 from 110 to 300 rubles a month. Pension expenditures were increased from 3 billion rubles in 1955 to 7.6 billion in 1961, thus aiding one of the lowest income groups. Reforms affecting the collective farms have diminished the huge discrepancy between the rich farms—those favored by nature or capital investment—and the many farms so poor they have been virtually outside the national economy. The State Committee on Labor and Wages, set up in 1955 to overhaul the incentive system—which as Deutscher has pointed out had become outmoded by changes in technology and labor skills to the point where it was virtually a *disincentive* system—raised pay rates systematically in the lowest grades. Khrushchev outlined the effort in his summary speech on the new program at the 22nd Congress:

It is common knowledge that on the initiative of the CPSU Central Committee much has been done in recent years to streamline wages. As a result of these measures the high incomes and salaries of some categories of staff have been considerably reduced. At the same time minimum wages have been increased. The bringing of the incomes of different categories of workers closer together has also been helped by the established procedure on the abolition of taxes on wages. In short, much has been done to reduce the gap in incomes between different groups of the population.[6]

The cutting of high incomes has been done with little fanfare, but this casual reference by Khrushchev is substantiated by reports from informal sources. Nicholas DeWitt gleaned a few pertinent facts from remarks by

official Soviet visitors to the United States, and has docu-
mented individual cuts of roughly 10 to 30 percent in
academic salaries—which are among the highest.* Wright
Miller, a perceptive British observer who has written a
very interesting book on the Russians, cites from his own
acquaintance: "In 1959 many of the highest salaries were
being cut by half—I heard of academic salaries reduced
from 20,000 to 10,000 rubles a month."[8] And from other
nonofficial sources we know of cuts in the 10 to 40 percent
range for the higher incomes.

The plans for the future point to a continuation of
these trends of equalization. Specific targets in the seven-
year plan that ends in 1965 indicate that there is to be a
rise in minimum monthly wages of between 65 and 100
percent. Altogether, it is planned to raise those in the low-
income brackets by 70 to 80 percent during the plan, while
the average increase for all categories is to be only 26
percent, thus concentrating most of the increase in money
wages at the poor end of the spectrum.[9]

For the decades of the sixties and seventies as a
whole, the aim is set by the new program as follows: "The
disparity between high and comparatively low incomes
must be steadily reduced. Increasingly greater numbers of
unskilled personnel will become skilled, and the diminish-
ing difference in proficiency and labor productivity will
be accompanied by a steady reduction of disparities in the
level of pay."[10] And Khrushchev: "Already, in the course

---

* Some reductions in 1958 monthly salaries compared with 1957: University professor in a science field without advanced degree, cut from
2,200 rubles to 1,900; director of a research institute of the Academy
of Sciences of the U. S. S. R. in a science field, cut from 5,000 to 3,500
rubles; the same, but a *personal* salary (as against a salary that goes with
the job) for a doctor of science, cut from 7,500 to 6,000 rubles; director
of a research institute of the Academy, doctor and corresponding member
of the Academy, cut from 5,100 to 4,500 rubles. The salaries remain
very high; they may be compared with a minimum wage at that time of
300 rubles, and an average of about 750.[7]

of the coming decade in the U. S. S. R., the task of historic significance, of the disappearance of the low-paid category of workers and employees will be resolved."[11]

But the Khrushchev regime, while pushing these measures, has resolutely defended the basic system of inequalities and so-called incentives, and bared its teeth when they are attacked, as they more frequently are nowadays. Sharply differentiated incomes, it is vehemently held, must continue all the way up to "the actual transition to communism." Khrushchev strongly rejected wage leveling in his address to the 22nd Congress on the new program, and in his reply to discussion, he put his point in polemical form, against "some comrades," unnamed:

I previously set out in detail the Party's plans in the field of production and people's well-being. But some comrades propose going considerably further than the outline plan and, in the near future, spreading the principle of free satisfaction of the requirements of the members of society to a wider sphere of material and cultural goods, to establish in fact equal remuneration for all without regard to qualifications and difficulty of their labor.

Such proposals are profoundly erroneous. Embarking upon such a road would be tantamount to undermining the material stimulus to raise labor productivity and put a brake upon the construction of communism. (*Applause*)[12]

Among economists, there are said to be some who favor dismantling the entire incentive system in favor of equalitarian payment. In a recent article in *Pravda*, the chairman of the State Committee on Labor and Wages attacked one A. Mandrugin for favoring the complete abolition of "the existing system of excessive personal incentives in the form of individual piecework payments."[13] But the official school of economists and party and government officials continue, in the description given by one leading economist, to favor only a "gradual curtailment of the differences of income," together with an increase in "the fund marked for joint satisfaction of needs." Only as greater abundance develops will there be the basis for a shift to distribution according to need, starting with "the objects of prime necessity used in greatest quantity."[14]

▲   ▲   ▲

Wright Miller delineates a large class of "leaders of Russian society" with specialized training and functions, higher incomes, and other distinctions.* His estimate of the size of this group may be too large, but the question he poses about them is vital:

The intelligentsia are thus a body of citizens, perhaps more than 20 million in number, whose social characteristics (apart from their functions) are still in a fluid and transitional state. It is impossible to say whether they will eventually be accepted as a privileged class or whether, with the raising of the standard of living all round, they will be integrated, as a merely more interesting group, into a kind of community not yet seen in any country. What happens will depend, as usual, partly on the Soviet Government and partly on the reactions of the Soviet people.[15]

The question posed here is, essentially, whether the Soviet Union has a chance of achieving that sort of classless society traditionally associated with the ideals of socialism.

* Mr. Miller's book provides an excellent description of the privileged strata, their relations with manual workers, distinctions in dress, absence of deference—a survey of factors on both sides of the picture of class divisions.

His answer, as any answer given now, is necessarily vague, but it can perhaps be supplemented by a listing of some of the forces at work.

In view of what has already been done, we cannot doubt either the will or the ability of the regime to scale down the most extravagant inequities and raise some of the lowest levels. But this is a far cry from preparing the groundwork for a fully equalitarian society, overcoming the resistance of a large, varied, and well-entrenched caste of privileged persons, which dominates the state administration and the economy, the military, and most of the other professions. Parts of this grouping may go along with reforms, and the rest may only grumble, but how will they react to threats against basic prerogatives? Such a situation in human affairs always has spelled political conflict, and there is little reason to think Russia is different in this regard—although we cannot yet be sure what forms it will take.

Those forces that will seek the complete dismantling of the system of privilege and will want to create what Wright Miller calls "a kind of community not yet seen in any country" exist only as scattered individuals whose names we know chiefly from the attacks against them. But we must not neglect the impact upon young people of the persistent teaching of equalitarianism as an ideal, even if a distant one. The Soviet privileged grouping is in the unique and anomalous position, among all the privileged groupings of history, that it must teach the nonlegitimacy of its own privileges and powers over society. By reason of history and ideology, it must either pretend these privileges do not exist, or argue in effect that its trusteeship over the society is temporary, as over a ward that has not yet come of age. As we have seen from the past decade of Soviet history, this ideology raises echoes among the young people, and will evoke greater ones in the future.

It is hard to accept the opinion of Klaus Mehnert, author of a West German book on Russia that has become a best-seller throughout Europe, that it would take a "state of real emergency" and sacrifice to start a new era of equalitarianism in Russia.[16] It seems more plausible that if any road to equality is possible, it is on the basis of abundance rather than a sharing of poverty. Where Soviet society will ultimately be led by the growth of great abundance combined with the continued teaching of socialist ideals, we cannot know. But if attempts are made to keep the present social structure, there is no question that it will lead to heresy and political dissent on a broad scale.

George Orwell has drawn us a picture of a society in which all thinking has become manipulative, and has no relation to actual events or social structures. Words come to mean their opposite, concepts deny the realities imposed on society. As an imaginative construction, *1984* enlarged certain things Orwell saw in the world around him at the time he wrote it, and it is both compelling and chilling.

But there is little reason to believe that such a society can exist outside the pages of literature. The idea that a ruling caste can teach its own nonexistence so effectively as to make the population under its heel disregard it, is intriguing but unrealistic. Rather, in teaching the non-legitimacy of privilege and dictatorial power, it undermines itself, particularly as other conditions ripen for the growth of dissatisfaction.

▲   ▲   ▲

We cannot close this discussion of equality and inequality without reference to the special matter of the
employment of women in the national economy. No feature of Soviet society is more startling, nor more significant in its implications for the structure of social institutions and the shape of future life in the Soviet Union than
the employment of women. As is well known, Russian
losses in the Second World War were so devastating that
the country has 20.8 million fewer males than females.[17]
It is a reasonable assumption often made in the West that
the widespread use of women's labor is in part due to this
fact, and in part due to the drive of the regime to use all
available labor power, male or female. We should also not
forget that the Soviet government, from its inception,
attempted to implement in several ways the long-standing
tradition of socialism that women have the right of equal
opportunity with men; badly scarred and distorted in application, this idea has not been without effect.*

The usual Western picture of the Soviet working
woman is that of the street sweeper. It is certainly true
that much unskilled labor is done by women in Russia:
wheeling barrows, carrying hods, spreading asphalt, carrying luggage, cleaning engines. As noted earlier, the surplus of women is concentrated in the rural areas, where
there are 17 million more women than men, and farm
women do much of the heavy labor required in agriculture. But we would be very mistaken to confine ourselves
to this aspect.

Some 68 percent of working-age women hold jobs
in the Soviet Union, as against 43 percent in the United

* John Gunther tells an anecdote about Khrushchev at a party:
"When a member of a visiting delegation commented on the fact that so
many Russian women work, Khrushchev horrified the guests by replying
cheerfully, 'Yes, our women work, and they are honest women—not like
women in France, who are all whores!' "[18]

States. Leaving aside the farms, women constitute some 47 percent of the labor force.

What is startling is that while women constitute 47 percent of the labor force, they make up 53 percent of all professionals in Soviet employment, and 65 percent of semiprofessionals. The term professionals includes of course such categories as teachers and librarians. It is not surprising to find that women hold some two-thirds of the jobs in this "educational-cultural" classification. We see something of this sort in many Western countries. It is a good deal more surprising, however, to find that three-quarters of all doctors (M.D. equivalent, not including nurses, laboratory technicians, etc.) are women—although this is a fact we have already heard repeatedly. But the facts about the other professions are more startling still. We know that there are women engineers, but it comes as a surprise to find that 30 percent of Russian engineers are women—and two-fifths of all agronomists, veterinarians, foresters; 60 percent of economists, statisticians, merchandising specialists; one-third of jurists; and 61 percent of all other professions!

Not that women are on a plane of full equality in these professions. They do not exercise a weight proportional to their employment in the professional specialties listed above. Nor do the Soviet state administration, the leading political bodies, the top party committees, show much evidence of women's equality. Despite this, there are some further surprises.

According to a compilation of "leading personnel"* in the professions, women do carry considerable front-line responsibility. For instance, in industry and related enterprises, women make up 40 percent of all employees

* A category of responsible and specialized jobholders defined by the Russian handbook *Women in the U. S. S. R.*, Moscow, 1960.

and workers. The proportion of women among "leading personnel" is 32 percent. Obviously this leaves something to be desired, and the picture becomes less favorable when it is focused on the topmost commanders in this and other fields. Yet, by comparison with conventional experience in most countries, what is significant is not the lag behind due proportional weight, but the extent to which women occupy positions of responsibility. It may be lamentable that women, making up 40 percent of Soviet industrial employment and 32 percent of all leading positions, hold only 10 percent of all top executive positions such as directors of enterprises and chief engineers, and only 14 percent of jobs as heads or deputy heads of shops. To most of us, however, these percentages are remarkable evidences of a distinctly different masculine-feminine relationship and hence of a distinctly different social structure.*

The large proportion of women in professional and semiprofessional employment shows that, besides performing much unskilled physical labor, women carry a very large measure of the mental labor of Soviet society on the most skilled levels and in the most traditionally male enclaves of industry and technology. Some of the professions most heavily staffed by women, such as medicine, are paid on a lower scale than in other parts of the world, either because women's income is taken to be supplementary for the family, or because these are regarded

---

* For other sectors of the economy, the picture is roughly similar. Women make up 66 percent of trade and distribution employment, and hold 46 percent of the leading jobs; they are 54 percent in government administration and economic management and planning, with 44 percent of leading jobs; 69 percent of all educational-cultural employment, 66 percent of leading jobs. In two areas, however, their proportion of leading jobs is higher than their proportion of employment: public health, where with 85 percent of employment they had 88 percent of leading jobs; and research and development in industry, where with 41 percent of employment they had 45 percent of leading jobs.

as altruistic and service professions. Still, there is no evidence that women are actually paid on a different scale from men for equal work, and there must be an extraordinary number of families where the woman holds an economic position fully equal to that of the man, and many in which her income and status are higher.

It is hard to overestimate the importance of these facts for the future of Soviet society. We need not call attention to the advantages the economy gets from fuller utilization of the talents and labor of the whole population, at a relatively minor cost in nurseries, kindergartens and extensive paid maternity leave. But there is no question that, in addition, all bourgeois family norms are undercut.

The Soviet leaders probably have primarily economic motives for this policy. They may in fact desire a "stable" and even bourgeois or Victorian family, as an aid to social stability. Certainly they have shown little evidence of a radical desire to break up the traditional family—boarding schools notwithstanding. But, like the plans for strengthening communal services, this trend too will weaken the family as it has traditionally existed.

In any case, one thing that emerges from the data on this subject is that if the Soviet Union does retain a stable family structure, it will not be able to do so, as a general rule, at the expense of the female of the species. In the employment picture that is developing, such subordination is no longer possible. The Russian woman is much closer to being free of her oppressive husband—a species overwhelmingly dominant in the old Russia—than to being free of an oppressive state.

As to what happens when the sexes begin to converse together as engineers, tool designers, or economists, we will not even try to conjecture about that. The Russians says it means the death of frivolity; the West says it means the death of romance. Certainly it will extend, beyond anything we have known in the Western countries, the modern trend toward feminine equality, with consequences that must affect every part of the society.

C H A P T E R   VIII

The Problem
of Soviet
Culture

The artistic temperament and the cultured mind have traditionally, in all revolutionary upheavals, been haunted by a great fear and inspired by a great hope. The fear is that turning a nation upside down will result in the destruction of the cultural heritage laboriously cultivated during centuries, and that the suppression of a privileged aristocracy will destroy the repository and patron of the creative arts and the best in culture. The hope is that the elemental disturbance in society will smash old traditions and formulas and have a liberating influence on the forms and content of expression, giving birth to a new age of human culture, more free and more advanced than the old.

The fears of cultural destruction, which shook even Bolshevik leaders like Lunacharsky and close sympathizers like Gorky at the time of the revolution, did not prove justified. Commissions for the protection of cultural treasures functioned from the early days, an extraordinary number of museums were set up to house Russia's vast

117

artistic inheritance, and even hated relics of clerical power were preserved for their historical and cultural significance. At the same time, artists in all fields were given support by the government, which in this way took the place of the aristocratic and bourgeois patrons of Czarist days. Institutes and training classes, theaters and houses of opera, music, and dance, were established and aided, and by every account have multiplied lavishly in the country, even in its most unlikely corners.

But if the fears were not fulfilled, neither were the hopes. After a promising period of free development, there came the virtual death of art. Every form of experimentation, honesty, spontaneity was either curtailed or entirely ended. Using stringent penalties, the regime decreed pompous styles and fatuous tones, forcing upon the artist a propagandist mission. By the thirties, the liberating impulse of the revolution in art had been crushed. The regime imposed such narrow limits upon the solution of the artistic problem, and the hypocrisy and barrenness of thought proved so stifling, that few noteworthy products emerged from the pens, brushes, cameras, and stages of Soviet artists, well endowed with patronage though they were.

It will not surprise us to recall that the abrupt reversal in the arts coincided with the start of the collectivization and industrialization campaigns. The new road and the harsh means chosen required that the turbulent spirit of the country be subdued, its unruly and searching inquiries be subordinated to the technical-mechanical process. Instead, the artists were called on to aid in the organization of the labor army, preach the virtues and successes of the regime, take part in the war against illiteracy, and help in every way they could. As in so many other realms, in this one too: the revolution succumbed so that the revolution might continue. Every other revolutionary feature was sacrificed to the effort to create an industrial nation suited to the doctrines of socialism, so that in carrying on its revolution in industry, Russia became the least revolutionary of countries in most other respects.

We thus arrive at the paradox that, for much of its history, the Soviet Union has been the guardian of the nineteenth century in art, propagating zealously the achievements of an earlier day and attempting formal imitations of styles that antedate the revolution by decades of time and eras of art evolution. Contrary to both fears and hopes, its aesthetic conservatism has been monumental. This, like so much else of the Stalin era, has a double aspect. No major culture of our time has been so impoverished and uninteresting in its original contributions, or in its lack of ability to reflect the excitements and experiments of our time. But neither has any been more successful in bringing to its population, on a mass scale, some of the best of the cultural heritage of mankind.*

In the process, characteristically, the dark and disquieting voices of the past, like Dostoevsky, were deemphasized. The emphasis was on optimism, progress, humanism. And although the regime boasted of a "new socialist humanism," it has as yet been little in evidence. The veneer of socialist phrases thinly veils an uncomplicated and smug, often Victorian outlook, which has taken over along with the confidence and optimism in nineteenth-century bourgeois thought—its rationalism and faith in the perfectibility of man—some of its most repel-

---

* "Yet—and this is the grand contradiction in the Soviet scheme of things—the prodigality with which the Soviets have made available the great literature of the past, Russian and foreign, is in staggering contrast to the restraints they have imposed on Soviet writers in their efforts to depict life as they observe it and portray character as they envision it." (Maurice Hindus, *House Without a Roof,* New York, 1961, p. 82.)

lent features—hypocrisy, prudery, timidity, a narrow horizon, and boastful self-satisfaction.

At the same time, the spread of serious literature in the population begins in the classroom and goes on even in the factory or collective-farm library. "Soviet education, even though it uses the humanities and the subjects directly related to the humanities for the indoctrination of communism, affords its students vastly more thorough training in these subjects than American schools afford our students," writes the author of a recent comparative study of the Soviet and American curriculums.[1]

The reading habits of the Soviet people seem to focus heavily on technical and educational literature studied for self-improvement and job advancement, in connection with extension, night, and correspondence classes. There is at the same time in the newly literate Soviet masses a vast and highly appealing involvement with the best of their own culture. The Russians are described as voracious readers, en masse, of Pushkin, Radishchev, Herzen, Tolstoy, Turgenev, etc., "a people enraptured by its national culture. . . . Sentiment aside, it is difficult for the westerner to conceive how a body of literature might so engage the consciousness of a people."[2]

"The great hunger for books," we are told by another observer, "is one of the most striking features of Soviet life, and the state seems to spare no effort to gratify it. The sidewalk booksellers almost rivaled in popularity the ice-cream and soda-water vendors. . . . There were no comic books on the sidewalk stalls, no Westerns, no paperbacks with gaudy illustrations of semi-nude, bosomy females. But there were Dickens and Galsworthy, Tolstoy and Chekhov and other classics, and Conan Doyle, whose immense popularity has begun to alarm the *Literaturnaya Gazeta*, Moscow's guardian of literary tastes and fashions."

This visitor comments: "That this literary inheritance from Russia's and the world's past has been made available to the Russian people on a gigantic scale has always seemed to me one of the splendid achievements of the Soviets."[3]

Klaus Mehnert has noted the same thing: printings of the classics (including, recently, Dostoevsky) sold out within a few days after publication in editions of hundreds of thousands and even millions, the crowded Moscow bookstalls, the absence of trivial and sensational reading, the "naïve enthusiasm and thirst for knowledge." He concludes that "an intense effort towards intellectual self-improvement still governs the pattern and rhythm of life. And, unless I misread the signs, it will continue to do so for many years to come."[4]

We need not describe here how the same spirit is characteristic of stage and ballet, of the poets—who bring out crowds of thousands in icy cold to hear open-air readings, and sell editions that are the wonder and envy of Western publishers—of the devotees of music, chess, dance, poetry, who follow their idols with the avidity of sports fans in the West and make popular heroes of them in much the same way. The dissemination of fine arts as a popular culture is evidently under way in the Soviet Union at a great pace; not so, however, the creation of a true, original, or penetrating artistic life of its own.

▲   ▲   ▲

Since Stalin's death and particularly since the publication of Ilya Ehrenburg's novel, *The Thaw,* in 1954—which was both a signal to millions at home and watchers abroad, and also gave the period its name—the artistic and literary community of Russia has been sharply divided into warring camps. Since the issues in the debate encompass basic questions of ideology, morality, and politics as well as strictly aesthetic questions, the debate naturally has great importance.[5] "Their split concerns the momentous question of how and where Russia should evolve after the national trauma symbolized in Stalingrad's becoming Volgograd," writes one Western observer.[6] "The outcome of the struggle will profoundly affect Moscow's relations with the West and the nature of internal evolution in the nation," writes another.[7]

It is natural for Western intellectuals to attach such import to signs of change among their opposite numbers in the East. Nevertheless, Soviet intellectuals, despite their privileged position, do not dominate their own country any more than the Western do theirs. It is hardly likely that the bitter conflict now being waged among Soviet artists and writers will resolve the fate of Soviet society. But it does have enormous significance nonetheless. These battles are an anticipation of clashes due to wrack all of Soviet society in the coming decades. Intellectuals, concerned chiefly with ideas, tend to feel the stirrings of impending social storms before others, who generally react when the crisis takes a more material form. Also important is the fact that the battle among the artists and writers is being fought almost entirely in the open, and hence adds substantially to our knowledge of the stirrings in the depths of Soviet society, especially among young people and students.

In the intense factional struggle that has flared repeatedly in the cultural organizations and periodicals, the big majority is reportedly on the liberal side. While the tides of battle have shifted from year to year, favoring now one group and now the other, on the whole the undeniable general trend has been toward more freedom.

Even if the liberals win, however, and achieve greater scope for experimentation and critical writings, the direction of Soviet art and literature is not thereby determined or made clear. The liberals are far from homogeneous in their approach. Some are intensely political, and want to use their pens not just to support communism but to criticize those features that seem to them to distort and strangle it. Others are disillusioned or confused by politics, and want to escape from it into a world of personal emotion. Some are extremely experimental; others, including Aleksandr Tvardovsky, the leader of the liberal grouping, are flatly conventional and content with traditional forms for themselves. Some, like Ehrenburg, are interested in the rehabilitation of personalities and schools destroyed in the Stalin era; others are concerned with their current problems. The unifying element seems to be little more than a demand for greater artistic autonomy and freedom of expression. This is certainly a valid platform for a liberalizing bloc, but it tells us little about the Soviet culture of the future.

As the external constraints loosen, the artistic world will be freer to assume its "natural" configuration. But what might that be? The prerevolutionary and pre-Stalin generation of experimentalists has long since passed from the scene, and in any event its specific approaches and solutions no longer apply. The role they might have played in fructifying later developments was cut short by the extirpation of their art and of many of them along with it. The present generation of artists was hand-picked and hand-raised by the regime, and their training, ideology, as well as what Abram Tertz calls their Purpose, were all supplied by the same source.[8] The younger gen-

eration, starting out in the fifties and sixties, takes shape
under somewhat newer and more free conditions, but we
do not really know as yet what they can do artistically, or
what they would like to do—as they themselves may not
yet know.

In reality, the dictatorship over Soviet art is only one of
the problems, and may be the most easily solved—or, let
us say, the soonest solved. The Soviet government found
it possible to survive a turbulent, inconoclastic, bitter,
satiric surge of art in the twenties, when the regime was
far weaker, and might be able to survive the artists' barbs
again today or tomorrow, when it is much stronger. Abram
Tertz insists that it is not just the imposed state policy
which has stultified development—and he makes that
point despite the fact that he himself had to publish his
remarkable essay, *On Socialist Realism*, under an assumed
name in the West, and certainly knows what the dictatorship is:

Art is not afraid of dictatorship, severity, repressions, or
even conservatism and clichés. When necessary, art can be
narrowly religious, dumbly governmental, devoid of individu-
ality—and yet good. We go into aesthetic raptures over the
stereotypes of Egyptian art, Russian icons and folklore. Art is
elastic enough to fit into any bed of Procrustes that history presents to it.[9]

If this leads us to think that Soviet art faces difficulties in finding its feet even if it should be set free, we
are probably right to think so. Of course there also are
bewildering confusions in the literature, painting, music,
and other arts of the West. But at least there is richness
and vitality of experimentation, and thus an absorbing
excitement. The urgent problem facing the Soviet artist

is that of coming to life under rather unprecendented social conditions.

The problem may be stated very generally: While a certain duality is inevitable, it is hard to visualize Soviet art separating into two distinct streams, one feeding the needs of a specialized and sophisticated stratum, and the other catering to mass needs. This is the sharp division characteristic of culture in the West today; the conditions of Soviet state and society make it unlikely that so sharp a cleavage will develop there. It is part of the artist's bargain with the state, part of the ethos of the society, that art be accessible to the mass. Within this context, the chief limitation on the artist will continue to be the general level of culture, education, and sophistication. Under such conditions it is hard for art to develop the subtle, symbolic, allusive, and elliptical styles, the daring, the profundity that it requires to mature.

In discussing this problem at the close of his massive study, *The Social History of Art,* Arnold Hauser points out that "there is today hardly any practicable way leading to a primitive and yet valuable art." The "violent simplification of art" is impossible; a genuine and creative art today must be a complicated one. Yet it is just this path of a "violent simplification" that the Soviets have tried to take. The solution, Hauser says, is to "extend the horizon of the masses as much as possible" by education, "training of the capacity for aesthetic judgment." This presupposes an advance on a broad front: "The preconditions of a slackening of the cultural monopoly are above all economic and social."[10]

Some will doubt the advent of such a Periclean Age; others will see it as a possibility. But I think all will have to agree that the conditions that inhibit Russian art—the nature of its position in society and the nature of its audience—will continue for some time to come. When we consider this, and when we consider also that Soviet culture is permeated with an optimism of progress which Western sophisticates find inexpressibly naïve and infinitely boring, it is clear that the gulf between Soviet and Western art will persist in the forseeable future. The Western aesthete may comprehend and perhaps appreciate the Soviet ambition to raise the cultural level of the mass, but given his attunement to the arcane techniques, discordant and despairing tones, and moral neutrality of his own modern art, he may find little to interest him coming out of Russia.

▲   ▲   ▲

The Soviet pretense of a revolution in art has as yet nothing to support it. True, one of the formal conditions for a new departure is present. The Soviet mind rejects the anxiety, alienation, and pessimism that form the mood underlying the frantic tempos and shattered forms of much of modern Western art. But its rejection has thus far been imposed chiefly by administrative fiat and coercion. It is thus truncated by its lack of mastery of the achievements which it would surpass, and lacks the wealth of experience to be gained only through the free play and natural evolution of styles. The new humanism it would develop is overshadowed by the hypocrisies it has practiced in defending the harsh requirements of industrial construction. Apart from occasional exceptions in the past and a fresh honesty to be seen developing today, its habit is to evade the ultimate realities of existence, drowning

them in conventional stereotypes or crippling them with
awkward and graceless presentations.

The regime has, at the same time, prevented the
development of a mass idiom on the Western model:
cheap sensationalism, scandalous journalism, trash on the
comic book level, inane pornography, and so forth. But it
must be remembered that this material fills a genuine need
in the West. Its culturally exploited consumers take it up
at an early age, turning away from the goody-goody
schoolbooks and lifeless fables for juveniles because they
find in the violent and salacious comics, the scandalous
newspaper and magazine stories of crime, passion, adul-
tery, greed, and hate, an echo of the lusts and disorders
of life as they witness it.

A true and living art must be rude to all shibboleths,
honest and realistic without fear of coarseness, vibrant
with the excitements of life as it is lived, not as it is ideally
envisioned, iconoclastic and questioning, tainted with human sins and weaknesses. Not having this, and not having
its mass Western substitute, the cultural life of the Soviet
Union is left with a great vacuum. The conventional tales
and morality fables, the idealized products that are encouraged, are not adequate to satisfy the healthy young
mind. There will be a rush to fill the vacuum. We have
already seen this, partly in an avidity on the part of some
young people for Western sensationalism, partly in a surge
toward the new young poets and playwrights who display
private passions, lyrical loves and bitter hates, unsparing
candor about their guilt, partly in an interest in modern
Western art.*

* A British observer of the Soviet scene writes: "In the West we are
uneasily conscious of the widening gap between highbrow and popular
culture; we may have doubts about the health of both, but there is
no denying that both on the whole satisfy their consumers. In the Soviet
Union there is a single, synthetic official culture, which makes a few

Thus we see the vacuum in Russian culture filled in various ways. Naturally, it would be best if the elements of good taste and maturity of mind instilled in the new Soviet generations by their training in excellent literature, together with the further development of Soviet society and culture, bring a victory of life in art in its best forms, and not in a cheap and meretricious ersatz entertainment. But in one form or another, now that the shackles are loosening, life will break through.

---

concessions to vulgar tastes and far fewer to those of the elite. It has no rotten spots; it is just dead. Ehrenburg has asked authority to recognize the existence of different levels of taste, and authority was unwise to reject his plea. As it is, both the uneducated and the elite are terribly vulnerable to foreign cultural influence."[11]

Is Democracy
Possible
in the
Soviet Union?

If Soviet economic and social institutions appear very crude when judged by the standards of socialism, in the political life of the U. S. S. R. the distance between slogan and reality is so great they are almost diametrically opposed. In Marxist theory, a country that attains social- ism enlarges the political democracy capitalism has achieved, by adding to it economic and social democracy. Although Russian ideologists make constant use of these Marxist categories, there is practically no reality to them. The idea that, in the industrialization drive the Soviet Union conducted, the country was organized as a socialist association of free and equal producers, is nothing less than fantastic. Rather the people were driven, herded, brutally whipped into the cities and compounds of the factory system. In doing this, all forms of free political life were destroyed by a dictatorship almost as complete as any in modern times.

In theory the Soviet state is a "dictatorship of the proletariat"—the working people organized as the ruling class and using the state to lay the foundations of a new social order. But as the workers themselves were subjected to the tyranny of the Stalin years, it was only by stretching Marxist ideas to their ultimate limits that such an idea could be upheld. In practice, the state raised itself so far above any form of control by society that if we try to use Marxist terms at all in defining it we must have recourse to Marx's concept of the "Bonapartist state," after the dictatorship of the Second Empire in France, when the state seemed "to have made itself completely independent."[1]

This phenomenon, of a state appearing strongest and most arbitrary just when it is divorced from the active support and direct participation of any of the classes of the population, so that it has apparently raised itself above society, always has a puzzling aspect. Its Soviet manifestation is no exception. It is beyond the scope of this book to try to solve the mechanics of this feat of levitation, so commonplace in our time that it has been seen in a great variety of social situations. Suffice it to say, however, that such a regime represents a condition of innate instability and tension, rather than the stability it seems to display. It may overcome its crises by increasingly unlimited use of force, but this very tendency is the hallmark of its instability, since no society can long endure in such a situation.

The end product has usually been some sort of debacle, whether in a revolutionary outburst, a foreign adventure, or internal breakup of the state power through separatism or annexations by other states. The Soviet Union, however, is a unique case, and some of these ordinary expectations do not readily apply—or apply in a very special way. If the political structure is ossified, the rest is not. Russian social and economic life is being revolutionized from top to bottom. Bertram Wolfe, in spite of his belief in what he has called "the durability of despotism in the Soviet system," has explained this point forcefully:

At first glance the word conservative may seem out of place in speaking of a society that is organized revolution. And indeed there is a striking difference between Communist totalitarianism and all previous systems of absolute, despotic, undivided (and in that sense, total) power. For whereas despotism, autocracy, and absolutism were bent on preserving the *status quo*, Communist totalitarianism is dedicated to "the future." This powerful institutional structure which tolerates no rival centers of organization has a vested interest in keeping things in flux. It maintains the omnipotence of its state and ideology by carrying on, within and by means of its power system, a permanent revolution. Like Alexander's, it is a revolution from above. Indeed, much more truly than Alexander's and much more sweepingly and exclusively is it a revolution from above. Its aim is nothing less than to keep society atomized and to create, as rapidly and as completely as the recalcitrant human material and the refractory surrounding world will permit, a new man, a new society, and a new world.[2]

It is the singular fate of Soviet totalitarianism to have brought into being a new country, within which it must try to preserve its powers. Thus instead of the more familiar situation where the absolutism of the regime brings about a crisis of the nation, in this case a transformation of the nation has brought a crisis of the regime.

The view that the transformation of Soviet social and economic conditions means "the twilight of totalitarianism" in the U. S. S. R. was pioneered by Isaac Deutscher, the biographer of Stalin and Trotsky and analyst of current Soviet affairs, who has advanced it cogently for more than a decade.[3] The thesis has drawn heavy fire from some quarters. In particular, Deutscher has been accused of making a simplistic equation between industrialization and democracy, and the example of Nazi Germany has been raised to show that "one of the most highly literate and technologically trained peoples in the history of man adopted Nazism when that people was both universally literate and possessed a high proportion of scientists, scholars, and persons with secondary school training."[4]

The longer one thinks about this argument, the harder it becomes to understand its relevance. Germany was certainly an advanced nation, but it was in a state of almost total social paralysis, economic crisis, and universal desperation when it fell victim to Nazism. It had been in a condition of breakdown for at least a decade and a half. Should Soviet social and economic institutions fall into a comparable state, few would venture to predict the outcome. But if we conceive of a general ascent of the Russian economy, the German example does not seem to apply at all.

In any event, it is time to bring to bear on this dispute the experience of the past decade. No one can doubt the sweep or seriousness of the changes in Russian political life since 1953. The basic mode of rule has in fact shifted away from terrorism; the institutions of political police, blood purge, slave labor camps, have been reduced to a fraction of their former place in the state structure. The mood of liberalization, with all its ups and downs, has encroached on the despotic controls in every field, from literature to economic science, from poetry to politics. If we do not attribute this to the successes of industrialization, the progress of education, the social and cultural revolution, and all the consequences that flow from these, we are left with only one thing to attribute them to: the magnanimity of Stalin's heirs. The latter view, historically untenable in any basic sense, is likely to meet with even greater resistance from Deutscher's critics than the former.

Rather than continue a largely fruitless and scholastic debate over whether democratization is "possible" in the Soviet Union, it is by this time more important to recognize the major trend, which appears to be beyond dispute. The mode of rule of the Stalin era proved not only unsuitable but unworkable as Soviet society developed in social and economic complexity, urban sophistication and educational standards, and as self-confident and resourceful new generations appeared on the scene. We may quarrel over such Marxist formulations as Marx's own "social existence determines consciousness," or more homemade emendations like Brecht's "Erst kommt das Fressen, dann kommt die Moral," or Khrushchev's famous "We are getting richer, and when a person has more to eat he gets more democratic." These are expressions of a theory which may or may not convince us. But in the past decade of Soviet experience we are confronted with a body of fact that stands superior to any theories, and when that happens it is better to reconsider theory than to disregard fact. What has now become more important than old debates is to discover what trends and tendencies emerge from a decade of the post-Stalin era, so that we can try to visualize the probable characteristics of the Russian political future as concretely as possible.

▲   ▲   ▲

Whereas in Eastern Europe the crack in the monolith definitely loosed strong sentiments of anticommunism, so far as can be judged this is not characteristic of the Soviet Union in the post-Stalin upheavals. To be sure, many incidents of discontent cannot be classified, as for example the reported uprisings in the concentration camps in the early fifties, or reports of strikes in Soviet factories. But insofar as a social and political platform has taken shape and found expression, it appears to aim at altering rather than overthrowing communism.

In the work of militant youthful ciritics like Yevtushenko, this even takes the form of a renewed spirit of dedication to communism, not merely ritual obeisance. In his work of mid-1962, "The City in the Morning," he describes his dissident role as that of a *protector* of communism:

> I am a Communist by nature
> And communism orders me
> Toward all that stands in its way
> And I will not be thrown off by advice.[5]

The regime is of course as vigilant as ever against anticommunist writings, and it may be objected that such opinions have in fact taken shape, but are unknown to us. This may be, and if they are there they will sooner or later become known. But we have the reports of many travelers who have gained the confidence of anonymous Russian friends, and these reports do not substantiate the idea that there is a feeling of opposition to the basic social and economic institutions, even where envy of better conditions in the West is expressed. Nor do we find an alternative to Soviet communism sought in the

underground literature we have from the Soviet Union—
writings "for the desk drawer" or for pseudonymous publication in the West. Abram Tertz, in his bitter little book,
is filled with revulsion against many features of his society,
but he does not think in terms of what we would call anticommunism. Czeslaw Milosz warns the reader in his introduction to the American edition:

> But American readers would be mistaken if they attrib-
> uted their own values and perspectives to this anonymous
> Russian writer, and regarded him as a supporter of the West-
> ern way of life, for instance. . . . If this anonymous Russian
> were asked whether he is a Communist or an anti-Communist,
> he would almost certainly shrug and answer: "What does that
> mean?" Only one kind of reality exists for him: it is that in
> which he has grown up and which forms his daily environ-
> ment. . . . He lives with the problems of his own commu-
> nity. . . .[6]

Any conclusion we can arrive at in this matter is of
course tentative and subject to verification as events proceed. But even a minimum of analysis shows that it is unlikely these preliminary signs will play us false. Even if
virtually every feature of modern Soviet life were to feel
the power of popular resentment and opposition in the
years to come, the economic, historical, social, juridical,
and psychological impossibility of dismantling the basic
structure of public ownership and substituting something
—what could it be?—on the order of Western property
relations should be manifest. The impossibility of a "res-
toration" means that, however modified by the shocks
of the coming decades, the Russian system is going to be
based on some variety of collective or government owner-

ship. The world has been irrevocably altered by the development on this new basis of a huge and growing industrial power.

▲　　▲　　▲

There has been no move in the direction of a political and ideological center outside of communism. Further, the Communist Party, instead of being virtually smashed, as in Hungary, by the post-Stalin upheaval, has maintained and even strengthened its position. In the last decade or more of Stalin's reign, the party had been waning, being relegated to the background in favor of other instruments of rule. It has now regained its central place. It has been the arena of de-Stalinization, debate, and intramural conflict. Although attempts to pit other institutions against it have been made, none has succeeded. There is every reason to believe that the key struggles to come will take place within that organization, and not in the conflict of institutions like the army, industry, police, party, against one another.

The Communist Party is in part a privileged caste, in part a governmental and administrative agency, but also in some considerable measure it is an actual political party that shares the familiar characteristics of such bodies. This means first of all that it is in some degree a political selection of people. The standards of membership, the way the party renews itself, require people willing to undertake a political role. The pledge of a party member is a vow of allegiance to the regime, and an active political life embodying both responsibility for the regime and the

enjoyment of its favors in the form of political and occu-
pational preferment. If the latter involves privileges, the
former is at times onerous and has been—in wartime—
hazardous.

In some ways the party is only a mutual-support
society whose object is to hold and enjoy power. But the
ties that unite it to certain basic goals are too intimate, too
strongly conditioned by history, and too closely bound
up with the training, traditions, and experience of its
members to be entirely disregarded. To think of it as
nothing more than a political freebooters' association is
to fly in the face of much that we know, and to render a
great deal of what happens in Russia inexplicable. While
political power is in the forefront of Communist preoccupation, this preoccupation is within the context of the modernization and industrialization of Russia and its transformation along bureaucratic-utopian lines.

In the years before its rise to power and the first decade of its rule, the party had a long record of internal
disputes and divisions testifying to the free play of opinion
among party members, which, while hardly absolute, was
in any case impressive. Lenin himself was often in a minor-
ity, and virtually every other Bolshevik leader of importance took positions opposing Lenin without suffering
thereby. The change in this respect came in the latter part
of the twenties, with Stalin's rise to power, and this change
was consolidated in blood in the purges of the thirties.

The party lost its own democratic life when it became
the instrument for the imposition of a rigid dictatorship in
the country. It could not remain, as it had hoped, an island
of democracy in a sea of dictatorship; the Bolsheviks could
not, in Deutscher's phrase, "abolish democratic rights for
society at large and preserve those rights for themselves
alone."[7]

Having achieved complete and terroristic ascendancy over the party by the start of the thirties, Stalin next proceeded to free himself from dependence upon it. One student of Russian communism has given this its most extreme formulation: " . . . we might say that the purge destroyed the Communist Party, although I know of no one who has expressed this fact so drastically. Nonetheless I believe it to be true. Not only did the Great Purge kill off or jail almost all those who had been members of the party before and during the revolution of 1917. In that sense, the party of Lenin certainly was destroyed. But in addition the place and function which the party had had in Soviet society was changed so drastically that we might speak of its destruction."[8]

Whether we accept this extreme formulation, or that of a leading historian of the party, who speaks merely of a "decline in the influence of the party," stemming from the "personal ascendancy of Stalin," "deliberately fostered in the interest of the safety which the dictator sought in the duplication of his instruments of control,"[9] the point is clear. Stalin ruled more and more through his personal secretariat and the secret police, bypassing party bodies with increasing frequency and often not even bothering to inform them of important decisions.

Of all the political shifts of the post-Stalin era, the most important has been the reversal of this trend. The liquidation of Stalin's personal secretariat and of the independent powers of the secret police, which followed on the heels of his death, were only the most dramatic incidents in this campaign. The history of the entire period is one of expansion of party powers and a prolonged effort to instill new life and vigor into the moribund party units, from the top of the pyramid to the bottom. The party has again been restored as the center of political life of the country, as can be seen by the all-important role played by the succession of party congresses from the 20th to the 22nd. Not only have the congresses and plenums of the Central Committee become far more frequent, but they have unquestionably become the centers of discussion and decision of basic policy questions. We even know of instances in which the Central Committee has become the court of appeal for settling clashes in the topmost body, the party presidium—at least one of these disputes, the attempt to remove Khrushchev from his post as First Secretary, involving a question of ultimate power in the state.

The return to a party-centered regime and the end of police dictatorship involve important consequences for the party. We have just seen the beginning, and we do not know where it will end. But at least at the outset the need is for greater initiative, energy, and spirit in the party bodies, if they are to be made use of as instruments of rule and inspiration throughout the country. Among the measures designed to provide this was the adoption at the 22nd Congress, along with the new program, of a new set of rules for the party.

By these rules the members of the presidium were limited to three successive terms in office, and for both this body and the Central Committee it was decreed that not less than one-quarter of their membership be renewed at every Congress. The same provisions were applied on a more drastic scale to lower party units, and were also laid down for nonparty governmental bodies, like the Soviets. An exception was made for "particular party workers" of "generally recognized authority and high political, organizational, and other abilities," who may retain office for further terms, providing they receive three-quarters of the votes instead of a simple majority.

In themselves these new rules may not mean much, as a high turnover of membership has been characteristic of the functioning of party bodies. So long as the party is controlled bureaucratically from the top down, they may only provide national and local secretaries with a convenient system for removals. The changes in the rules, however, taken as a whole, show a considerable effort to revivify the party through the granting of greater scope to members and greater checks on officials. The adoption of the rules was preceded by a discussion in the party journals, including many letters from members proposing more liberal modifications than those adopted. Kozlov, in his report to the Congress, noted that questions had even been raised about the long-standing prohibition of factions.[10] This discussion, in the view of one Western expert, "was rather more open and frank than any similar discussion in the party press had been for a long time. . . . It is plain that there is a growing demand in the lower and younger ranks of the party for greater decency and greater democracy, for less manipulation, less dishonesty, and less dictatorship."[11] This analyst, in a study comparing the new rules with the old ones, finds changes along the following lines: The rights of free discussion and criticism for members are more broadly defined; the duties are more comprehensively listed, with great stress on the ethical code for Communists, their concern for public welfare, abnegation of careerism, dishonesty, and greed; expulsion of members is made somewhat harder, but lower units are now given the right to recommend disciplinary action against any member of a higher body (a move that was expressly prohibited in the old rules). These and other changes he summarizes as an attempt to instill new life and enthusiasm into the party, and meet "the widespread pressure at the lower levels for greater democracy."[12]

▲   ▲   ▲

As Russia enters new political waters we do not really know what is going on in the minds of the rank and file of the Soviet populace. Western opportunities for finding this out are limited. The traveler who makes his way to the Soviet Union is generally not in contact with factory employees even in his own country, let alone in Russia. He is limited not only in his interest, but in his ability to gain the confidence of such people or to understand and interpret their hopes and fears. Thus while we have many interesting reports of contacts with Soviet artists, journalists, scientists, administrators, for the general population all we have is an occasional Western report of a talk with a Moscow cabdriver (the cabbie is everywhere taken to be *vox populi* for the simple reason that he is one of the few working people that middle- or upper-class persons meet—and he seems never averse to playing oracle). The Harvard Project on the Soviet Social System did try to fill this deficiency, but the interviews and questionnaires it amassed from Soviet refugees in 1950 and 1951 dealt with the Soviet Union of the first years of the forties, when these refugees were washed out by the tides of war. It is thus badly dated, besides suffering from the usual defects of sociology-by-questionnaire.

One Russian told an American friend that in the year following the 22nd Congress, where Stalin's crimes were given a mass airing for the first time and when Stalin's body was removed from public display in Lenin's tomb, "the people learned to talk all over again." This American summarizes her impressions by saying that "out of the pain, disillusion, and anger, out of loss of faith on which the lives of the Soviet people were founded, something positive has begun to take shape: public opinion."[13]

Such a formation of public opinion runs counter to the trend of some decades, when all but official opinion was shattered and suppressed. Its function as a check on the rulers, a guarantee against re-Stalinization, and an independent force for further change can be of the greatest importance in coming decades, especially as it takes on national scope, political coloration, and the boldness to express itself in meetings and periodicals. Signs exist that this last trend has already begun in letters to the editor and in local meetings.

Among the mass of the population the most elementary conditions of political life were, at the start of the Khrushchev era, entirely absent. The people were politically atomized, lacking any form of independent organization, still in a state of shock from the sufferings of the industrialization drive, the war, and the postwar reconstruction, and could have little perspective on the problems of the country. All dissident leadership among them had long since been wiped out.

In these conditions it is understandable that the political pressures would find their earliest outlets through the elite of Soviet society. Despite their privileges, specialists, administrators, professionals, and intellectuals had an immediate stake in change insofar as the old rules and conditions made the performance of their functions difficult or impossible, rendered their condition precarious, or clashed with ideals sincerely held. In general a ferment of the elite has been characteristic of the Khrushchev era thus far. In itself the initiative from above is no surprise.

But from this decade of change what stands out is this: the Soviet elite is far from being a homogeneous body. It includes varying interests, outlooks, sympathies. It is likely to divide in periods of severe stress. In fact, it has already divided repeatedly, in conflicts over agriculture, industrial management and planning, foreign policy, de-Stalinization, economic science, and literature. In some cases, the arguments have been muffled and confined. In others, as for example the debates over economics, the conflict is openly conducted in the press. In at least one case—literature—the leaders in the field have divided into tight factional schools, each with its spokesmen, periodicals, and following among writers and readers. The shattering effect of the anti-Stalin revelations and the breakup of monolithic dogma are hastening this process. We can expect the further appearance of differences, tendencies, and group alignments in the Soviet leadership; rather than a solid phalanx confronting the subject population as a unified conservative force, the ruling group will show rifts which are likely to aid the ferment.

▲   ▲   ▲

It is an article of faith in the West—or at least in the United States—that a democratic society cannot be based upon a nationalized and state-controlled economy. It takes the pluralism of scattered holdings, the diversity of interests, the multiplicity of havens for the individual offered by a privately owned economy, to provide a workable basis for freedom. The concentration of economic power in the hands of the government—no matter how well intentioned—inevitably means a totalitarian political and social structure.

That this argument seems natural and ineluctable is a consequence of the entire course of American political history. In the United States, democracy has indeed been a federalism of contending interests from the start. The Union was founded as a compact between states, sections, classes. On one occasion the compact was broken by an appeal to arms, but traumatic as the Civil War experience was, it has not destroyed either the method or national confidence in it. The federation of regions and interests, working out its conflicts through balancing and reconciling, remains fundamental to the American idea. It is from this that our whole conception of democracy as compromise, horse-trading, arbitration, has emerged, and the idea of a democracy based on a different foundation seems strange and unlikely.

Since the social and economic framework created over the last forty years in Russia is entirely different, there is in my opinion little possibility that the Russians will develop a democracy of this type. In their society the play of antagonistic interests is necessarily subject to a larger framework of economic planning. The system does not and cannot allow free activity to diverse interests, limited only by their clashes where they impinge on each other. It is not just that such a method would threaten the workings of the economy; more properly, the economy would be unworkable on such a basis. Naturally in this as in all other societies there is much room and occasion for compromise and conciliation, for partial solutions and arbitration. But, speaking generally, it is apparent that we are dealing with a far more unitary structure.

If a Soviet democracy is possible, it probably cannot be based upon a loose federalism of contending forces comparable to that of the United States and other Western countries. It will have to be based more upon a community of interest than on a reconciliation of diverse interests. These are two very different foundations. The Soviet effort is obviously far more ambitious and difficult than the Western, presupposing as it does a harmonious society rather than a fractionalized one. It is hard to imagine the contours and workings of such a democracy, as few models for it have existed, and those only partial and limited. Essentially a self-governing community of free associated individuals, a vast co-operative in which each has a share, stake, responsibility, rights, it would be chiefly distinguished by a strong element of social cohesiveness: the feelings and obligations of community.

The very unitary nature of Russian society and the necessarily demanding character of a democracy based upon a community of interests places it far out of reach in the next few decades. Its prospects hinge upon the successful fulfillment of all the promises of Soviet life and the defeat of all the social hazards that loom. This gives such a democracy so speculative and remote a character that it actually belongs to a different order of social evolution from that of the present epoch, demanding as it does a society rid of tensions, fully in control of its material and cultural problems, and more harmonious than we can at present envisage. But this does not mean that Russia cannot achieve a much greater measure of freedom than it now has within the coming decades. Given a continuation of the present trend, not only is that possible but highly likely.

To visualize this more concretely, however, one salient question must be considered. The major element of political freedom is its exercise. Political freedom cannot really be "granted," as in the Stalin Constitution of 1936, even if more sincerely given and allowed. It does not exist until it is successfully used. Can a grouping arise in Russia which, with a critical view of the dominant political power, will yet be able to exist and propagate its views? That would be the turning point. And in my opinion it is not impossible that we will see within the next period informal alignments of leaders, periodicals, party followers, with dissenting viewpoints. Should these produce a grouping, whether through a split in the present leading bodies or an upthrust of new young leaders, strong enough to make its suppression a difficult matter, compromises with it, along the lines of the 1956 Gomulka compromise in Poland, are not out of the question.

In some ways, this is the logic of everything that has been happening. The divisions among Communists on the international scene are the portent. Similarly, the dividing of Communists within Russia, which, tentatively, has already been happening, leads toward the revival of a true political life for the country, although in the first instance confined to the Communist Party.

▲   ▲   ▲

The regime took millions of *muzhiks,* unaccustomed to disciplined work or even regular hours, ignorant, slothful, superstitious, illiterate, and transformed them into industrial workers, technicians, scientists, administrators, office workers—everything a rapidly growing modern society requires. The transformation was quick and brutal in the extreme, and depended on the will of a handful of leaders.

From this long experience there emerged a tutelary relationship between leaders and led, regime and subjects. It is habitual on both sides, and will not be easily broken. But while it remains largely comfortable for the leaders, it is becoming irksome for the led. The restiveness, the precarious ideological position of the trustees of power, the policy divisions that are bound to appear in the leading committees and the consequent search for popular support, the remodeling of the whole society along more enlightened lines—all these things point to the likelihood of some form of democratic development in Soviet society during the next few decades. The possibility of the realization of a co-operative democracy on an entirely new model, superior to the forms of democracy hitherto known, is, despite Russian claims, so remote that it can be discussed at this date only in the most speculative way. But lesser changes, including the formation of a tradition of civil liberties, the opening of an area of limited but licit political dissent and debate, and the appearance of wings and factions of opinion—even if loosely organized and informal—may not be so very far in the future.

Socialism

and

Communism

In a short manuscript written in 1875, *Critique of the Gotha Program,* Marx directed his attention briefly to some of the characteristics of the society he believed would succeed capitalism. Normally reluctant, he was drawn into this discussion by his disagreements with the specifications for the new society set forth by the congress of the German Social Democrats held at Gotha in that year to unify the two wings of the socialist movement.

In trying to clarify the rather muddled vision projected in the Gotha program, and in trying to give the question a historical and evolutionary form in place of an artificial one, he distinguished between the immediate postcapitalist society and the subsequent stage. First, there is the society "as it *emerges* from capitalist society; which is thus in every respect, economically, morally and intellectually, still stamped with the birthmarks of the old society from whose womb it emerges."[1] This he divided from the later stage which has transcended these "birth-

marks" and "has *developed* on its own foundations," which
he sketched briefly as follows:

In a higher phase of communist society, after the enslaving subordination of individuals under division of labor,
and therewith also the antithesis between mental and physical
labor, has vanished; after labor, from a mere means of life, has
itself become the prime necessity of life; after the productive
forces have also increased with the all-round development of
the individual, and all the springs of co-operative wealth flow
more abundantly—only then can the narrow horizon of
bourgeois right be fully left behind and society inscribe on its
banners: from each according to his ability, to each according
to his needs![2]

On the basis of this evolutionary distinction between
the immediate postcapitalist society and the later one
which has "*developed* on its own foundations," Marxists
speak of the "lower" and "higher" phases of communism,
more usually called, respectively, socialism and communism.

For the first two decades of the Russian revolution
no one thought to call Russia a socialist society, except
in the loosest political parlance. All of its own leaders
understood that even though it possessed some of the
formal characteristics in the shape of government ownership of the means of production, it was a special case, not
discussed by Marx. It was not really a postcapitalist society
(in Marx's words, "as it *emerges* from capitalist society");
it had to *reproduce* capitalist society, in its own peculiar
way.

But in the mid-thirties, less than a decade after the
industrialization drive had begun, with the country in
turmoil, the farm system shattered by collectivization, a
frightful political terror in progress, Stalin decreed that

socialism had already been achieved. From that time to the present, this has been the dogma. Seizing upon Marx's comments about the continued existence of inequality and other "birthmarks" of the old system, Soviet ideologues justified their claim to having achieved socialism chiefly on grounds of a continued resemblance to capitalism in the form of the wage system, commodity production, private farming, and so forth. On the basis of such a line of argument, of course, the more a country is like capitalism, the more it is socialist. They neglected the chief prerequisite hitherto understood by Marxism: that the society stand upon the shoulders of mankind's best previous achievements, and thus be economically, culturally, morally at least a match for capitalism—an elementary proviso fitting in naturally with the idea that socialism would come first in the most advanced countries.

Nevertheless, this dogma was proclaimed. The necessary consequence was that discussions about the transition to communism inevitably began. In terms of the Russian reality, this was entirely fanciful; a little bit like discussing sainthood for a man who is not even in a state of grace. But the discussion continues on that basis to this day, a heritage of the Stalinist era of boastfulness and of pasting fantastic labels on still crude institutions.

The new program adopted by the 22nd Congress proclaims the achievement of communism, in its main aspects, in twenty years: "Thus, *a communist society will in the main be built in the U. S. S. R.*" by 1980. "The construction of communist society will be fully completed in the subsequent period."[3] On the basis of the foregoing considerations, this claim need not detain us for long. The prospect of a communist society is still beyond any visible horizon in the modern world, and, as we have been discussing Russian prospects throughout this book, depends essentially on the chance of surpassing capitalism in a number of fields, and thereby organizing an industrial society on a distinctive basis, with new possibilities.

If we leave labels aside, however, and discuss the possibility of achieving the concrete aims of the twenty-year plan, we can arrive at some important conclusions. As we have seen, many of the economic aims are practicable, in purely arithmetic terms. The prospect of altering institutions, however, as we saw in our discussion of the Soviet state and culture, is a more difficult matter. In these areas, perspectives are limited by the cramped vision of the men in power (and, as yet, of the society as a whole), and even these limited visions are complicated by the tensions between program and reality. We find this to be true in the case of the various institutional changes projected in the so-called transition to communism: the end of commodity production, the abolition of income classes along with the abolition of pay differences used as incentives, and so on. Khrushchev very properly ridiculed Stalin's theory that the way to the withering away of the state was the continual strengthening of the state, which would grow harsher as class tensions lessened. But, for a number of reasons, we find the present leaders falling into the same difficulty.

Let us take as an example the simplest economic category, the commodity. In Marxist terms, the value attached to a commodity under capitalism is a reflection if its share in the total social labor; it is exchanged for other commodities, and the relation between men is transformed into a relation between things. In a postcapitalist society, Marx repeatedly stressed, the economic relations between men would be direct, and not expressed through relations between commodities.

The dying out of commodity relations and their replacement by direct social accounting is necessarily a lengthy process. In the Soviet Union, however, the trend is in the opposite direction. Commodity relations were poorly developed at the outset, and they have been getting stronger. As a result, Soviet economists have engaged for many years in a great discussion about whether commodity relations—as well as other capitalist categories—ought to exist under socialism, and if they should, whether as a natural part of the system or as an excrescence upon it.

From the point of view of Marxism, the answers to these questions should be quite clear and simple. But the Soviet economists, led by Stalin, confronted, and still confront today, a number of difficulties. In the first place, commodity relations exist, and Russia has already been defined as having achieved socialism. Second, commodity relations are urgently required by the regime for its economic policies. The outcome was therefore predictable: Kronrod, one of Russia's leading economists, has formulated it this way: first, commodity relations are not due to the "underdeveloped" character of socialist relations, they are a true part of socialism; second, "since commodity relations are immanent to socialist production, they are developed as socialism is developed"; third, throughout the socialist era we may therefore expect the "development of commodity relations rather than their curtailment"; and fourth, commodity production is eliminated, with its causes, only in the final transition to the second phase, full communism.[4]

This curious analysis, which is also advanced to cover other elements of the transitional society that the Soviet Union is supposed to eliminate only two decades from now, elements such as inequality, pay incentives, and so on, is clearly the result of a practical contradiction. Many devices which clash directly with the vision of a co-operative society, a "New Soviet Man," and a new institutional structure, are still badly needed to stimulate production: this premise, on the basis of present operations, is quite correct. The next premise, that all plans for the future society hinge on the vast expansion of production, is also correct. From these premises the conclusion unavoidably flows that in order to achieve communism, some of the very elements of social and economic life which communism aims to abolish must be broadened and entrenched more deeply in the present system.

The Soviet theorists confront this contradiction unblinkingly, since they have the magic word "dialectics" which enables them to resolve contradictions. Such "dialectical contradictions" are not only unsurprising to them, but even comforting. They have not stopped to think that when societies make their way forward through contradictions, when institutions which at one stage facilitate progress later stand in its way, these contradictions are, according to their own theory, resolved by clashes between entrenched interests and fresh forces of progress. The "incentive pay" system, for example, fosters both a privileged grouping and the selfish social habits of inequality, which pervade the population at large. By entrenching this abstract-sounding economic category in the society, the regime deepens some very concrete forces—which influence and perhaps subjugate the regime itself. The transition to new forms will thus hardly be a matter of decree. The stage is being set for social struggles—in part by a tension of interests and in part by a tension between institutions and ideology.

▲   ▲   ▲

Communism, as Khrushchev told the 22nd Congress, is an age-old dream of mankind. Plato, Andreae, Bacon, Campanella, More, Wells, Morris, Bellamy, and many others have drawn pictures of harmonious societies, peopled by emancipated men and women organized for rational and co-operative endeavor, freed for the full development of their intellectual, physical, and moral faculties. This dream was passed on from ancient sources through French socialism to Marxism, whence it has become the institutionalized purpose of Soviet society.

While discussion of communism in anything like its traditional vision is fanciful in Russia today, the goal and the discussions around it play an enormous role in Soviet society. Through it, an ideal is firmly implanted in the minds of millions, thereby intensifying the morale and unity of the country. A national goal that will bring benefits to all, predicated on community endeavor, becomes bound up with each day's work, and gives a transcendent significance to routine efforts.

The habit of judging all present endeavors in the light of the most demanding and visionary national purpose ever set by an entire country has dynamic implications. It will play an immense role in the shaping of new political and social opinions. As the setting for present debates, it is used to some degree to dampen current discontents with future promises. But it also implants great expectations. To think of the program merely as a set of promises the regime has no intention of keeping is to miss the point entirely. First of all, we have no basis to conclude that the regime views its own perspectives dishonestly, as a gigantic confidence game. Second, it takes little reflection to see the extreme dangers of such a game and its inevitable consequences not many years from now.

Rapid industrialization gives Russia most of its dynamism, but much of it is also inherent in ideology. As new perspectives, new possibilities, new resources, and new experiences broaden the Soviet horizon both for rulers and ruled, dogmatic ideology will be superseded by visions both more concrete and more ambitious. Debates and conflicts will modify some parts of the map to the future, and explode other parts. In all of this, the role played by the discussion of the "transition to communism," as we have already seen in the past few years, will be central.

▲ ▲ ▲

Russia is obviously in transition to something; the question is what? Some have concluded that Russia is at last on the road to socialism. This was implied by Deutscher a decade ago in a discussion of Stalin's final article, *Economic Problems of Socialism in the U. S. S. R.*, when he closed his analysis with the words: "Stalin had intended to give the 'young cadres' the measure of the great distance which separates Soviet society from communism and to indicate in what way that distance might be shortened. What he has actually indicated is, in Marxist terms, the distance that still separates the Soviet Union not from communism but from socialism."[5]

The same point has recently been developed by George Lichtheim in his essay on the new Soviet Communist Party program. " . . . the mere fact," he argues, "that the central core of the document relates to the need for rapid economic growth under conditions of intensive rationalization and mechanization would be enough to discredit the claim that what we have here is a blueprint for a Communist society. What we have in fact is a prospectus for a state-controlled system, with a fast rate of growth and a planned economy; in other words, a Socialist society in the precise sense of the term."[6]

The force of this idea increases as we survey the conditions that will have been created at the end of two decades if the program is even moderately successful. Basic industrialization will have been completed and agriculture will have been modernized, and the country will have an immense productive plant. The living standards of capitalism today will probably have been equaled and possibly have been exceeded; the bottom layers of extreme poverty, so stubborn in every society hitherto known, may have been entirely eliminated. The revolution in education and general culture will have transformed the nation; here standards in excess of anything known under capitalism are likely. To these things we must add the beginnings of a new form of distribution through communal services. The spread between income classes will be somewhat lessened, and greater freedom for dissent and a variety of political expression will have appeared, although we cannot be sure how far this will have gone.

All of this will occur within the framework of a state-managed economy. Elements of a market economy—commodity exchange, incentive pay, monetary and credit relations, planning through competitive profit accounting, etc.—will not only continue but may be strengthened and broadened in their application during the long drive for productivity that still lies ahead. Planning will still be central and bureaucratically administered, in the sense that the planners' scale of requirements, and not that of communities or individuals, will dominate (although it may not clash, at all points, with the latter). The present characteristics of work, with the "enslaving subordination under division of labor" that Marx spoke of, and the "antithesis between mental and physical labor," will still exist, although doubtless ameliorated by technical progress; the population will remain divided into social layers.

The catalogue could be continued, but it is evident that even as described by the program, the successful completion of the projected construction would in general finish the creation of an immediate postcapitalist society. Russia has taken a special path, but what will she end up with in the next decade? It will be a society as it might appear if, after having passed through capitalism and enjoyed a vast technological revolution bringing high living and cultural standards, it abolished its capitalist institutions, nationalized the economy, instituted a series of broad welfare programs of major scope, and prepared to develop society further on this new basis. If this is what Russia does have at the end of two decades, socialism is exactly what it ought to be called in Marxist terminology.

Indeed, as Lichtheim points out,[7] the new program "recognizes in an oblique fashion" that the aim is not communism but socialism when it says: "The main economic task of the Party and the Soviet people is to create *the material and technical basis of communism* within two decades."[8] This, in Marxist terms, is nothing but another name for socialism.

Conceived in this way, the long prehistory of Russian socialism is coming to an end, and its proper history as a new form of society instead of an *ad hoc* construction is just about to begin. In the decades to come the Russians themselves may reconstitute for the world the image of socialism which their own development shattered.

C H A P T E R   XI

Conclusion

It should be evident that the chief problem of Soviet society is not a directly economic one. The Soviet Union is in an economic race with the United States, and barring a war or some other unforeseen major development, the outcome of that race is a foregone conclusion. The associate director of the Harvard Russian Research Center has reminded us: "What is most difficult for us to face is this: that events do not appear to have contradicted the conviction of the Soviet leaders that their directed economy has competitive advantages over the free market economy of the West in an age of advanced industrialism."[1] Difficult or not, this is a fact that the West must learn to face. The smug assumption that the Soviet Union has fallen into a hopeless mess from which it can extricate itself only by imitating the West is not well founded. As a matter of fact, from a strictly economic point of view, the Soviet system has fewer problems and stronger perspectives than the capitalist economies.

The chief problem is that in undergoing its remarkable combined development, skipping over capitalism, Russia skipped over much else that was painfully accumulated in the bourgeois era. The traditions of humanism, tolerance, respect for the individual, the experiences of a multiparty system and parliamentary democracy—these things may not be the ultimates of human development but they had been expected by Marxism to serve as the basis for further evolution.

Instead, Russia's first forty years of a "substitute bourgeois era" have witnessed unchecked despotism, rampant fear, extreme dogma, and other pressures that virtually wiped out the moral norms in political life. The gap represents not just an absence of certain Western experiences, but the presence of evil habits that became second nature for several decades. We can see much promise in the abandonment of many of the worst methods during the past decade, and in the shame with which present-day Russia looks back on its recent past. But this is far from enough. There is still no coherent view of Russia's history, no realistic picture of the causes of the shameful past, and most important, there is no moral and ethical map to the future comparable to the economic perspective.

The Soviet Union has yet to develop a code of ethics in the dealings of the community with the individual at least as good as that of capitalism, let alone better—or, to put it another way, at least as good as its social welfare programs. And Russia, with its greatly expanded state power, needs this even more than the West. While the industrial conquests of the bourgeois era can be duplicated or exceeded by sheer technical means, the subtler and more delicate conquests of the law, the social code, the rights of the individual, cannot be bludgeoned into existence. To "exceed the narrow horizon of bourgeois right" in Marx's words, without ever having enjoyed it, is impossible in a

160

single leap. We may be sure that it will involve much confused scrambling and many tentative and insecure footholds.[2]

▲   ▲   ▲

In the foregoing pages I have presented little more than a framework for thinking about the Soviet Union. As in every abstract picture, concrete realities are replaced by ideas of them. Much firsthand investigation, the opportunities for which are not yet available to Westerners and cannot yet be honestly exploited by Soviet social scientists, is required to fill in this outline.

Yet it is impossible to think seriously about any large social phenomenon without using abstractions and reducing the multiplicity of events to a co-ordinated and simplified view. In doing this, much is necessarily omitted and oversimplified; one cannot hope to reconstruct actuality, only elements of a guide to it.

All thinking about Russia takes place within the framework of some sort of conception. The official Soviet self-appraisal, echoed by some uncritical supporters in the West, is one of essential harmony, co-operative progress, and movement from perfection toward something better. That at least had been the view until recent years, when a more realistic tone began to replace this blissful picture. In the West the most extreme view is that of Russia as the modern antichrist, working unmitigated evil without respite.

The most characteristic Western view of the Soviet Union sees it as a fixed and immobile dictatorship which will never change until compelled to do so by an external force. Although I have tried to maintain a balance of realism about the possibilities of Soviet development, my feeling is that this picture is not only wrong but completely inverted. It appears to me that of all the major societies of the world, Soviet society is the one that is *most* likely to undergo great changes in the decades to come.

Too much attention has been concentrated upon the minds and motivations of the Soviet rulers, and too little upon the imperatives of a civilization in reconstruction. Trying to determine whether the moves toward liberalization of the past decade were "freely granted" or "wrung from a reluctant dictatorship" is an unrewarding game; its practitioners may not settle much even if they succeed in answering this question. The convenient thing about the mind of a ruling elite is that it is just like anyone else's mind: one can find there anything one chooses. Kremlinology, as it is practiced today, is thus an exercise in projection or rationalization, and—all the more so in the absence of reliable information—far from the realistic analysis it hopes to be. For a long-term projection, the enormous possibilities and explosive tensions are far more to the point.

All the big questions about Russia's future can actually be condensed into a single question: Has the revolution that began in 1917 ended? has it exhausted its possibilities? can it go no further? If we answer this affirmatively, we are in essence saying that the Russian social structure has found its permanent shape—at least for the foreseeable future. Should this be the case, we may still expect some remarkable things from Russia, but many of its great potentialities will be eradicated and many of its great achievements soured by the dictatorship over political, cultural, and social life.

There are, however, sure indications that Soviet society cannot maintain its present forms. Its own rapid progress and intense change cannot allow it to settle down within the structure—still essentially intact—inherited from the Stalin era. And the need for change to catch up with progress is only part of the picture. Marxism and the impulse of the revolution of 1917 still remain, embodied in official ideology, spurring the nation on in manifold ways.

We have the lessons of the Khrushchev Interregnum to back this up. Many have discerned throughout the past decade the elements of relaxation, the subsiding of the wave, a hope to settle down and enjoy the new stability, prosperity, and tranquillity. These are present, in strong reaction against the headlong pace of industrialization and the painful effects of war and political terror. They show themselves in a revulsion against politics and purposiveness, and in a demand for consumer goods and Western comforts. But for some years it has been evident that these are subordinate elements, and have been overridden by a strong dynamism. The Khrushchev leadership has succeeded in imposing a great new effort—under much easier conditions and with much greater immediate rewards, but comparable to industrialization nevertheless. If the new twenty-year program weighs heavily on the spirit of the nation, we have yet to hear of it; rather, it seems by every account to have released a new vigor and *élan*.

We must conclude that the revolution is still going on, and that it will not come to an end until the nation assumes a shape in which the tensions between progress and backwardness, society and individual, idealization and reality, have been released. Meanwhile, these are the drives that power Soviet progress, and change will continue to be rapid until they subside and the country can sink to the slower and more evolutionary pace common to most countries in normal times.

In forging thus ahead, with its unusual institutional equipment and visionary hopes, the Soviet Union is beginning to enter *terra incognita*. In what has gone before, the nation found a new way through old terrain; in what is to come, uncharted lands will be traversed. With whatever reluctance, advanced Western society will be compelled to watch the Soviet development with new interest: Russia will become important not just as antagonist, but as a full-length portrait of a modern industrial society organized according to basically different principles. Russia has much to learn from the West. But Russia may also, at a later stage, have an impact on the West greater than can now be foreseen.

Notes

Chapter I

1. Marshall D. Shulman, "Beyond the Containment Policy," *World Politics*, Vol. 10; reprinted in Inkeles and Geiger, eds., *Soviet Society: A Book of Readings*, Boston, 1961, p. 672.

2. Isaac Deutscher, *The Great Contest*, New York and London, 1960, Chapter I.

Chapter II

1. *Capital*, Vol. I, London and New York, 1930 (Everyman's Library edition), p. 654.

2. Quoted in Alexander Eckstein, "The Background of Soviet Economic Performance," in Inkeles and Geiger, eds., *Soviet Society: A Book of Readings*, Boston, 1961, p. 310.

3. Raymond W. Goldsmith in *Employment, Growth, and Price Levels*, Hearings before the Joint Economic Committee, Congress of the United States, April, 1959.

4. Abram Bergson, *The Real National Income of Soviet Russia Since 1928*, Cambridge, Mass., 1961, p. 216. Professor Bergson's study, perhaps the most important of its kind, was financed by the RAND Corporation and is the culmination of nearly two decades of work.

5. Naum Jasny, "Interpreting Soviet Statistics," in Inkeles and Geiger, eds., *op. cit.*, p. 306.

6. Robert W. Campbell, *Soviet Economic Power*, Cambridge, Mass., 1960, p. 153; Morris Bornstein, "A Comparison of Soviet and United States National Product," in Joint Economic Committee, Congress of the United States, *Comparisons of the United States and Soviet Economies*, Part II, p. 382; also Gerhard Colm assisted by Joel Darmstadter, "Evaluation of the Soviet Economic Threat," same source, p. 535. The foregoing all agree in assigning some 25 percent of Soviet gross product to gross investment. Bergson gives a higher estimate, almost 28 percent.

7. Walter Galenson, *Labor Productivity in Soviet and American Industry*, New York, 1954.

8. Campbell, *op. cit.*, pp. 63–65.

9. Based upon figures supplied by Nicholas DeWitt, the specialist in Soviet education and professional manpower, in Bergson, *op. cit.*, p. 293.

10. Naum Jasny, "Plan and Superplan," *Survey*, October, 1961, pp. 29–43; reprinted in book form, *The Future of Communist Society*, New York, 1962.

11. Naum Jasny, "Interpreting Soviet Statistics," in Inkeles and Geiger, eds., *op. cit.*, p. 306.

12. *Survey*, October, 1961, pp. 190–191.

13. *Ibid.*, p. 9.

14. Rudolf Schlesinger, "The CPSU Programme: The Conception of Communism," *Soviet Studies*, April, 1962, p. 385.

15. Rush V. Greenslade, "Forward to Communism?," *Problems of Communism*, January-February, 1962, pp. 36–42.

16. August 5, 1961.

17. August 14, 1961.

18. Campbell, *op. cit.*, pp. 189–198.

19. Bornstein, *op. cit.*, pp. 391, 394.

20. Colm, *op. cit.*, p. 533.

21. Bergson, *op. cit.*, p. 295.

22. Allen W. Dulles in *Comparisons of the United States and Soviet Economies*, Hearings before the Joint Economic Committee, Congress of the United States, Part I.

23. Harry Schwartz, *The Red Phoenix*, New York, 1961, p. 170.

24. Harry Schwartz, "Reflections on the Economic Race," in Joint Economic Committee, Congress of the United States, *Comparisons of the United States and Soviet Economies*, Part III, p. 612.

CHAPTER III

1. *New York Times*, April 26, 1962.

2. Campbell, *Soviet Economic Power*, p. 71.

3. For information on Soviet soil and climate, see: Chauncy D. Harris, "Industrial and Agricultural Resources," in Inkeles and Geiger, eds., *Soviet Society: A Book of Readings*, pp. 9–12; Fritz Baade, *The Race to the Year 2000*, New York, 1962, pp. 64 ff.; Theodore Shabad, *New York Times*, February 18, 1962.

4. Naum Jasny, "Plan and Superplan," in Laqueur and Labedz, *The Future of Communist Society*, New York, 1962, p. 32.

5. Cited in Campbell, *op. cit.*, p. 75.

6. Nicholas DeWitt, *Education and Professional Employment in the U. S. S. R.*, Washington, 1961, p. 491.

7. Vermont Royster, *Journey Through the Soviet Union*, New York, 1962, pp. 23–24.

8. Alec Nove, *The Soviet Economy: An Introduction,* New York, 1961, p. 148.

9. *Ibid.,* p. 29.

10. Arcadius Kahan, "Recent Trends in Soviet Farm Incomes," *Problems of Communism,* November-December, 1961.

11. Campbell, *op. cit.,* p. 75.

CHAPTER IV

1. Hans Heymann, Jr., "Problems of Soviet-United States Comparisons," Joint Economic Committee, Congress of the United States, *Comparisons of the United States and Soviet Economies,* Part I, p. 1.

2. *New York Times,* November 24, 1962.

3. Campbell, *Soviet Economic Power,* pp. 120 ff.; David Granick, *The Red Executive,* New York, 1960, pp. 108 ff.; Nove, *The Soviet Economy,* pp. 160–161.

4. Speech of October 17, 1961, in Schwartz, ed., *Russia Enters the 1960's,* documents of the 22nd Congress, Philadelphia and New York, 1962, pp. 197–198.

5. *Ibid.,* p. 194.

6. *Ibid.,* p. 196.

7. *Ibid.,* p. 273.

8. Joseph S. Berliner, "Managerial Incentives and Decision-making: A Comparison of the United States and the Soviet Union," Joint Economic Committee, Congress of the United States, *Comparisons of the United States and Soviet Economies,* Part I, p. 366.

9. Speech of October 18, 1961, in Schwartz, ed., *op. cit.,* pp. 259, 261.

10. Speech of October 24, 1961, in Schwartz, ed., *op. cit.,* pp. 70–71.

11. *New York Times,* December 18, 1961.

12. Alec Nove, "The Industrial Planning System: Reforms in Prospect," *Soviet Studies,* July, 1962, pp. 1–15.

CHAPTER V

1. Abram Bergson, *The Real National Income of Soviet Russia Since 1928,* Cambridge, Mass., 1961, pp. 237, 245.

2. *Ibid.,* p. 152.

3. *Ibid.,* p. 237.

4. *Ibid.,* pp. 237, 245.

5. This symposium has been reprinted in Abraham Brumberg, ed., *Russia Under Khrushchev,* an anthology from *Problems of Communism,* New York, 1962, pp. 571–615.

6. Bergson, *op. cit.*, pp. 294, 297. See also Campbell, *Soviet Economic Power*, p. 161.

7. Wright Miller, *Russians As People*, New York, 1961, p. 195.

8. Speech of October 18, 1961, in Schwartz, ed., *Russia Enters the 1960's*, pp. 239, 246.

9. Speech of October 17, 1961, in Schwartz, ed., *op. cit.*, p. 190.

10. Lynn Turgeon, "Levels of Living, Wages and Prices in the Soviet and United States Economies," Joint Economic Committee, Congress of the United States, *Comparisons of the United States and Soviet Economies*, Part I, p. 320.

11. Quoted in *Problems of Communism*, September-October, 1962, pp. 12–13.

12. "The Background of Soviet Economic Performance," in Inkeles and Geiger, eds., *Soviet Society*, p. 310.

CHAPTER VI

1. Speech of October 20, 1961, in Schwartz, ed., *Russia Enters the 1960's*, pp. 45–53.

2. Stalin, *Economic Problems of Socialism in the U. S. S. R.*, New York, 1952.

3. Schwartz, ed., *op. cit.*, p. 51.

4. Deutscher, *The Great Contest*, New York and London, 1960.

5. Schwartz, ed., *op. cit.*, p. 51.

6. Alec Nove, "Toward a 'Communist Welfare State'?," *Problems of Communism*, January-February, 1960, reprinted with comments by others in Brumberg, ed., *Russia Under Khrushchev*, New York, 1962, pp. 571–615.

7. Lynn Turgeon, "Levels of Living, Wages, and Prices in the Soviet and United States Economies," p. 319.

8. *Program of the Communist Party of the Soviet Union*, New York, 1961, pp. 95–96.

9. *Ibid.*, pp. 100–101.

10. *Ibid.*, p. 101.

11. Speech of October 18, 1961, in Schwartz, ed., *op. cit.*, p. 257.

12. *Program*, p. 102.

13. Theodore H. White, *The Making of the President 1960*, New York, 1961, p. 143.

CHAPTER VII

1. R. H. Tawney, *Equality*, 1931, available in paperbound edition, New York, 1961, Chapter IV.

2. Wright Miller, *Russians As People*, New York, 1961, pp. 135–136.

3. *New York Times*, February 27, 1962.

4. Viktor Rozov, *Never Too Young*.

5. *New York Times,* February 8, 1962.

6. Speech of October 18, 1961, in Schwartz, ed., *Russia Enters the 1960's,* p. 278.

7. Nicholas DeWitt, *Education and Professional Employment in the U.S.S.R.,* Washington, 1961, p. 811.

8. Miller, *op. cit.,* p. 132.

9. Lynn Turgeon, "Levels of Living, Wages, and Prices in the Soviet and United States Economies," p. 324.

10. *Program of the Communist Party of the Soviet Union,* New York, 1961, p. 95.

11. Speech of October 18, 1961, in Schwartz, ed., *op. cit.,* p. 256.

12. *Ibid.,* pp. 256, 277–278.

13. Aleksandr P. Volkov, *Pravda,* April 4, 1962, reported in *New York Times,* April 5, 1962.

14. L. M. Gatovsky, at a meeting of the Social Sciences Departments of the Academy of Sciences of the U. S. S. R. in Moscow in June, 1958, translated in *Problems of Economics,* New York, January, 1959.

15. Miller, *op. cit.,* p. 144.

16. Klaus Mehnert, *Soviet Man and His World,* New York, 1962, pp. 75–76.

17. This figure is for 1958. The statistical data in this discussion of women's employment is from the materials collected in DeWitt, *op. cit.,* Chapter VI.

18. John Gunther, *Inside Russia Today,* New York, 1962, p. 110.

CHAPTER VIII

1. Arthur Trace, *What Ivan Knows That Johnny Doesn't,* New York, 1961, p. 4.

2. Patricia Blake, "The Heirs of Russia's Past," *The Reporter,* July 20, 1961.

3. Maurice Hindus, *House Without a Roof,* New York, 1961, pp. 40, 99–100.

4. Klaus Mehnert, *Soviet Man and His World,* New York, 1962, pp. 139, 155.

5. For informative summaries of the people, publications, and issues in this struggle see: David Burg, "The 'Cold War' on the Literary Front," *Problems of Communism,* July-August, 1962; Peter Viereck, "The Split Personality of Soviet Literature," *The Reporter,* March 15, 1962; Max Hayward, "Soviet Literature in the Doldrums," *Problems of Communism,* July-August, 1959; Harrison Salisbury, "Soviet 'Liberals' Fighting Neo-Stalinists for Power," *New York Times,* February 6, 1962.

6. Peter Viereck, *op. cit.*

7. Salisbury, *op. cit.*

8. Abram Tertz (pseud.), *On Socialist Realism*, New York, 1961, pp. 26.

9. *Ibid*, p. 89.

10. Arnold Hauser, *The Social History of Art*, New York, 1958, Vol. 4, p. 259.

11. David Allchurch, "Diversions and Distractions," *Soviet Survey*, October-December, 1958.

Chapter IX

1. Karl Marx, *The Eighteenth Brumaire of Louis Bonaparte*, Moscow, 1934, p. 108.

2. Bertram D. Wolfe, "The Durability of Despotism in the Soviet System," *Communist Totalitarianism*, Boston, 1961, p. 275.

3. See especially *Russia: What Next?*, New York, 1953; *Russia in Transition*, New York, 1960; *The Great Contest*, New York and London, 1960.

4. Bertram Wolfe, *op. cit.*, p. 651.

5. *New York Times*, July 18,1962.

6. Abram Tertz, *On Socialist Realism*, pp. 8–9.

7. Deutscher, *The Prophet Unarmed*, London, New York, and Toronto, 1959, p. 16.

8. Alfred G. Meyer, *Communism*, New York, 1960, p. 82.

9. Leonard Schapiro, *The Communist Party of the Soviet Union*, New York, 1960, p. 549.

10. Frol R. Kozlov, Speech of October 28, 1961, in Schwartz, ed., *Russia Enters the 1960's*, p. 139.

11. Leonard Schapiro, "The Party's New Rules," *Problems of Communism*, January-February, 1962, pp. 29–30.

12. *Ibid.*, p. 36.

13. Priscilla Johnson, "Old Terror and New Doubts," *The Reporter*, December 6, 1962.

Chapter X

1. Karl Marx, *Critique of the Gotha Program*, New York, 1938, p. 8.

2. *Ibid.*, p. 10.

3. *Program of the Communist Party of the Soviet Union*, p. 70 (italics in original).

4. Ya. Kronrod, "Commodity Production Under Socialism," *Problems of Economics*, a journal of translations, New York, February, 1959.

5. Deutscher, *Russia in Transition*, p. 160.

6. Lichtheim, "Reality and Experience," *Dissent*, Summer, 1962, p. 282.

7. *Ibid.*, pp. 282–283.

8. *Program*, p. 71 (italics in original).

Chapter XI

1. Marshall D. Shulman, "Beyond the Containment Policy," in Inkeles and Geiger, eds., *Soviet Society,* p. 671.

2. For an interesting discussion of Soviet and Western ethical tenets and their relations to each other, see Herbert Marcuse, *Soviet Marxism: A Critical Analysis,* New York, 1961, Part II.

Index